Strength Ball Training

SECOND EDITION

Lorne Goldenberg

Peter Twist

HUMAN KINETICS

Library of Congress Cataloging-in-Publication Data

Goldenberg, Lorne, 1962-
  Strength ball training / Lorne Goldenberg, Peter Twist. -- 2nd ed.
    p. cm.
  Includes bibliographical references.
  ISBN-13: 978-0-7360-6697-6 (soft cover)
  ISBN-10: 0-7360-6697-7 (soft cover)
  1. Weight training. 2. Exercise. 3. Balls (Sporting goods)
I. Twist, Peter, 1963- II. Title.
  GV484.G65 2006
  613.7'1--dc22

                                    2006026867

ISBN-10: 0-7360-6697-7
ISBN-13: 978-0-7360-6697-6

Acquisitions Editor: Martin Barnard; **Developmental Editor:** Leigh Keylock; **Assistant Editor:** Christine Horger; **Copyeditor:** Jan Feeney; **Graphic Designer:** Nancy Rasmus; **Graphic Artists:** Sandra Meier and Tara Welsch; **Photo Manager:** Brenda Williams; **Cover Designer:** Keith Blomberg; **Photographer (cover):** Tom Roberts; **Photographer (interior):** Brenda Williams; **Art Manager:** Kelly Hendren; **Illustrator:** Tom Roberts; **Printer:** United Graphics

Human Kinetics books are available at special discounts for bulk purchase. Special editions or book excerpts can also be created to specification. For details, contact the Special Sales Manager at Human Kinetics.

Printed in the United States of America

Printed in the United States of America   10 9 8 7

The paper in this book is certified under a sustainable forestry program.

Human Kinetics
Web site: www.HumanKinetics.com

United States: Human Kinetics
P.O. Box 5076
Champaign, IL 61825-5076
800-747-4457
e-mail: humank@hkusa.com

Canada: Human Kinetics
475 Devonshire Road, Unit 100
Windsor, ON N8Y 2L5
800-465-7301 (in Canada only)
e-mail: info@hkcanada.com

Europe: Human Kinetics
107 Bradford Road
Stanningley
Leeds LS28 6AT, United Kingdom
+44 (0)113 255 5665
e-mail: hk@hkeurope.com

Australia: Human Kinetics
57A Price Avenue
Lower Mitcham, South Australia 5062
08 8372 0999
e-mail: info@hkaustralia.com

New Zealand: Human Kinetics
P.O. Box 80
Torrens Park, South Australia 5062
0800 222 062
e-mail: info@hknewzealand.com

Strength Ball Training is dedicated to my mom, Shirley Twist, because she filled me with enough strength to stay inspired for a lifetime. The value of connecting with people who give energy and removing people who suck energy came from observing my mom in life, who boosted up everyone around her.

Peter Twist

Contents

Acknowledgments

Very few people in the business world or sports have been successful without the help and dedication of others. In my personal experience, I have been blessed with friends and business associates who have been integral to the success of my career.

The person who has had the most impact on my career path is Jacques Martin, Head Coach and General Manager of the Florida Panthers. In 1987, he provided me with an opportunity for my first NHL job. Since that time he has not only presented me with additional opportunities, but has demonstrated to me the necessary requirements for success in sport and business: perseverance, dedication, understanding, and commitment. Jacques was the jump-start for my professional career and continues to be the successful and respected professional I aspire to be.

When I met Gary Roberts of the Florida Panthers in 1985, he was a 17-year-old player who did not understand how conditioning could contribute to success on the ice. I was able to convince him that if he worked hard, it would pay dividends in his hockey future. Gary gave me my first opportunity to work with a player headed for the NHL; this opportunity has developed into a great working relationship and lasting friendship that has spanned over 20 years. His hard work and perseverance are examples that every player should live by. This hard work has led him to be recognized as one as one of the best-conditioned players in the NHL.

Lori Armstrong, vice president of business operations, and Janice Hodgins, office administrator, at Strength Tek Fitness & Wellness Consultants are my lifeline to my business. Without them I would not have the luxury to complete projects such as this book and DVD or travel to conferences to share my ideas and knowledge with others in the industry. They are the real backbone of my business, and my sincere appreciation goes out to them, and all the Strength Tek staff for being the best in the industry; we would not be where we are without all of you.

My coaches at the Athletic Conditioning Center, Adam Douglas and John Zahab in particular, who are not only great coaches but excellent exercise innovators who have contributed greatly to the increased content of this book. Our many athletes at ACC such as NHLers Daniel Alfredsson, Wade Redden, Freddie Brathwaite, and Jason York; CFLers Pat Woodcock, Scott Gordon, and Mike McCullough; and the thousands of amateur athletes who have believed in what I am trying to do for their development.

The University of Ottawa provided me with the knowledge for an understanding of the human body and the drive to the never-ending challenge of education.

My coauthor Peter Twist, who has helped me professionally and personally with many important issues over the last number of years, is the consummate professional, a wealth of knowledge, and a breath of fresh air in an industry that can sometimes lack the ability to share ideas and information. Thanks to other industry professionals such as Chris Poirier from Perform Better, who provided me with many opportunities to speak at his educational seminars to spread the word about strength ball training.

Matt Shearer and Rich Marks from UnderArmour Canada for providing me with the best training gear on the market for our photo shoot and DVD. UnderArmour can even make an old coach like myself look good well into his 40s.

Most importantly, to my two children Isaak and Danielle, who are very patient with Dad while he is away on work projects, I love you both! We now have many more exercises for you both to try.

Lorne Goldenberg

There are many inspirational people in the academic, fitness, and sport circles. Two noteworthy people who continue to lead their fields are Dr. Greg Anderson and Douglas Brooks. Dr. Anderson conducts research, delivers lectures, and as someone who grew up a gifted athlete, transfers his knowledge to the practical exercise setting. Greg is a Twist Master Coach who has shared his knowledge in formal settings and over many a beer to the benefit of our training paradigm.

Douglas Brooks influences the field with his countless texts and articles on personal training and high energy presentations to thousands of fitness professionals. His professionalism and positive attitude sets the tone for professionals in any field; his zest for life and abilities in adventure sports redefine age. Appreciation to David Weck and Fitness Quest, for inventing and providing a new stability ball innovation—the BOSU DSL stability ball, and for communicating on exercise ideas.

Fitness models Gerard Recio, Julie Rogers, and Arielle Nash, all from the Twist Conditioning team, gave top energy and concentration to ace every single exercise. They are great athletes, top coaches, tremendous educators, and smart sport business people who allowed themselves to be called "fitness models" for this project! Their physical abilities and exercise knowledge made the book and DVD shoots a snap—and a lot of fun!

Still others from Twist Conditioning contributed to this project. Brynne Elliott searched and reviewed current research, while Gerard Recio, Dean Shiels, Mason Gratto, and Lisa Northrup carefully edited the details of each exercise. Many eyes and minds make a book clean and accurate.

I would like to acknowledge the Twist Conditioning team overall; talented professionals and wonderful people who are passionate about making a positive impact in fitness and sport through exercise product supply, hands-on training, delivering education and certifications, and setting up others to successfully run training facilities. Their positive energy makes the journey enjoyable and whatever-it-takes attitude leads to impactful, high-quality results. Thanks to the Twist product team for providing all of the training products and to the Vancouver Twist Athlete Conditioning Center for locking off the space for a week to shoot the photos and DVD.

Andrew Clark, Twist Conditioning's VP of Education, and Dean Shiels, VP of Athlete Training Services, deserve mention for their longstanding influence on the quality of our training and education platforms. Janice Hutton is another consummate professional who has shared knowledge and advice from her experience as an athlete, coach, trainer, educator, and business person. I would like to thank Lorne Goldenberg for his longstanding friendship, his leadership in the industry, and his generosity to share sport science, exercise, and business information. Like many others, I have learned much from him.

Importantly, I would like to thank Human Kinetics, who always puts out a first class educational product. In particular, developmental editor Leigh Keylock and trade division director Jason Muzinic, who were instrumental in turning our words and exercises into a polished book format, and video producer Doug Fink, whose leadership and class made the DVD shoot a great experience with strong results. As a reader of so many of their other book titles, I appreciate the opportunity to also be an author for Human Kinetics.

Last but noteworthy, my daughters Zoe and Mackenzie for their heartwarming smiles and making me jump on the trampoline the minute I get home... and to my four-legged kids Rico and Loosy for logging so many energizing miles together in the mountains, snowshoeing, trail running, and hiking. Great spirits.

Peter Twist

Introduction

Since the publication of the first edition of *Strength Ball Training*, there has been a significant increase in the use of stability balls and medicine balls in fitness programs. Participants reacted favorably to the natural athletic feel of strength ball training, which is different from the mechanical nature of muscle isolation techniques. The integration of whole-body strength training with core, balance, and coordination training spawned an audience of trainers, coaches, and participants asking for more. Our response is *Strength Ball Training, Second Edition*.

Training with strength balls has had an immense impact on the fitness industry. Personal trainers needed specialized education to coach whole-body coordination and advance their teaching skills beyond what was required for selectorized weight machines. Training became more portable, allowing exercise specialists to take clients outdoors. Coaches could bring exercises right into their sport environment—on the court, on the field, or at the rink. Retailers noticed increased demand for these products. Where else can you find an exercise device you can use in your home that can give you thousands of variations of exercises without the need for a huge, expensive line of equipment?

To appreciate the power of strength ball training, you must only understand that your body functions as a unit, with muscles firing sequentially to produce the desired movement. Some muscles contract to produce movement, others contract to balance the body, and others contract to stabilize the spine and hold it in a safe position. Other muscles kick in each time your body recognizes a shift in position or to correct an error, such as a loss of balance. Your body is a linked system that coordinates athletic actions. Throwing a football requires the leg, torso, and upper-body muscles to work together and contract in the correct sequence. Your body functions as a linked system in everyday life as well, such as when bending over to pick up a baby and lifting the baby overhead to produce a smile. This movement is dependent on leg, torso, and upper-body strength—both prime movers and stabilizing muscles. This is the foundation for what we present in the second edition of *Strength Ball Training*.

Over the years, we have improved our strength programs by adding multijoint, full-body exercises with free weights that incorporate the entire body, dumbbell lifts while standing on one leg, and medicine ball drills to activate the entire body. However, the most versatile tool has proved to be the stability ball. Strength training with a stability ball offers an exciting breakthrough. The opportunity to make the body function as a unit to execute an exercise has tremendous utility in sport performance, adult functional fitness, kids' training, injury rehabilitation, and fitness for aging populations. Most important, you train with an unstable (round) surface. Strength and balance are summoned in unstable and unpredictable environments—such as when slipping on icy stairs, lunging to catch a falling child, and withstanding a check to continue running while catching a lacrosse ball. These real-life conditions require contributions from all muscle groups. Each joint and muscle senses position in space and changes to other linked joints and muscles to react and produce the appropriate action. This linked system is a kinetic chain that produces functional movement safely.

The stability ball exercises in this book integrate instability into the closed kinetic chain through prone and supine positions that build from the center of the body to the periphery. Medicine ball drills add a dynamic load that requires full-body, coordinated actions. Catching a weighted ball outside your midline trains the deceleration and responsiveness properties of muscles, placing emphasis on the core and posterior chain. Together these tools produce improvements that support athletic movements (such as skiing down a mountain) and full-body everyday activities (such as digging in a garden), which keep the muscles and joints healthy and reduce the risk of injury. It is really about training and integrating the body as a whole and taking the focus away from development of only the muscles you can see in the mirror.

Stability balls and medicine balls are making a positive contribution to the sport rehabilitation, athletic conditioning, and general fitness fields. However, as with all exercise, well-executed technique produces optimal results, while poor technique at best produces nothing and at worst causes injury. Although balancing and moving on a ball or catching and throwing a weighted ball seem like simple and playful concepts, activating your body's proprioceptive mechanisms and challenging your low back and deep abdominal stabilizers are serious undertakings. Since primary goals include improvement of posture, movement mechanics, and athletic skill, an illustrative book demonstrating effective exercises and proper technique is long overdue. In this book you will find the answers to your questions. To enhance the second edition, we have included an integrated DVD. This medium will provide you with an opportunity to view some of the more difficult exercises so that you can actually see the intricate movement execution for these exercises. Now there will be no excuse for improper exercise technique. Coaches, trainers, therapists, and self-guided fitness enthusiasts alike can follow the exercise progressions and modifications to customize each exercise for their level. It is important to know simple modifications for each exercise to make them easier or harder. When you first begin, you will most likely need to simplify certain exercises so they require a little less strength or coordination to make them appropriate to your level, to produce results, and to stay safe and injury free. You also improve with training, so eventually you will need to know how to change an exercise to make it more challenging and to require more strength and coordination.

The bottom line in real life and sport is that you are only as strong as your weakest link. For most people this is core, or torso, strength. How many people do you know with low-back pain? How many athletes have experienced abdominal, hip flexor, and groin strains? Strong legs and strong arms along with a weak core are an injury in the waiting. Strength ball training builds from the core out to the periphery, accommodating your upper and lower body while turning your core into your strength. A stronger core is your speed center and strength center. Most movements are initiated and supported with the core muscles, and this is not just your superficial six-pack muscles. It also includes more important muscles deep in the abdominal wall that protect your spine and stabilize movement. The demand of swinging a golf club is a perfect example. A golf swing is mostly core, a little legs, and even less upper body.

You will note the importance of building strength that is transferable to sport and everyday activities. It is safe to say that in the sporting world, golfers require the lowest amount of fitness of most athletes. A high percentage of golfers lack the core strength to be their best. Most have experienced back pain. If they work out, many rely on floor-based sit-ups, stationary bikes, and selectorized weight machines that isolate specific muscles. Ironically, golfers use high-velocity rotation in a standing position 70 to 100 times per round. In addition to the high-velocity rotations, golfers load only one side of the body by swinging the club in one direction, which contributes to many of the problems they have as they become injured. Golfers need excellent core stability and strength in the legs and hips for powerful rotation. You need to choose an exercise style that will prepare you for the specific task to be performed.

While many other sports use rotation for skill execution—throwing and kicking a ball, swinging a racket—they also need smart and reactive muscles for agility, balance, quick direction changes, body contact, falling, jumping, bounding, and many other athletic attributes. For athletes, the goal of strength ball training is to teach the body to move more skillfully. For functional fitness, incorporating whole-body stability and balance into an exercise increases the metabolic costs, causing you to expend many more calories as you build strength.

In 2002 when the first edition of *Strength Ball Training* came out, we used the general research pertaining to balance and the nervous system to justify the use of training we had long known to be beneficial. There were few documented studies at that time to justify the use of stability and medicine balls in training programs. It seems that research is constantly lagging behind the practical coaching of today's leading exercise practitioners. Forward-thinking strength and conditioning coaches are constantly finding methods and tools to take their clients and athletes to a higher level, sometimes to the chagrin of the researchers. There was a coach who said that if he had to wait for those with PhDs to justify with documented studies what he was doing in the training room, he would have to wait almost a full Olympic cycle before his methods were validated by science, rather than by the gold medals his athletes were winning.

Many traditional practitioners are skeptical of anything beyond an Olympic bar and a dumbbell. Some scientists are locked into periodization paradigms borrowed from Eastern bloc countries in the 1950s, defensive of any advancement that does not align with the model in which they have invested their career. We recommend being confident in one's knowledge yet also humble, because it is a fluid process in which we always strive to find new methods to generate better real-life results. This statement is more of a commentary on a progressive period of exercise development rather than a negative view of research. As the authors of *Strength Ball Training*, we both come from a background in science. As an exercise physiologist and conditioning coaches, we have lived in the academic research world and continue to be active in research today. We have been prudent in designing exercises that are founded on solid scientific principles, anatomy, neurophysiology, and biomechanics. But it is noteworthy that our pace of developing new methods of training is faster than the ability of science to validate the utility.

Since 2002 several researchers have had an opportunity to catch up to the practitioners and test some of the training methods and products. Some interesting research validates the use of stability balls in training programs, which you can find in chapters 1 and 2 of this book. You can also read about requisite stable strength exercises you should be able to complete before progressing to many of the unstable drills presented in this edition of *Strength Ball Training*. We present advice on selecting appropriate equipment as well as the general rules about making each exercise more or less difficult. Within each specific exercise are recommendations you can follow, including progressions (such as adding weight, decreasing the base of support, or increasing the speed of movement). In addition to each progression within a single exercise, the order of exercises in each section progresses from simpler moves to more difficult ones. We think these guidelines will add value to your program, help you enjoy the exercises, and produce the best results.

The DVD reinforces the written and pictorial instructions from the book for some of the more difficult exercises. Within the exercise chapters you will notice a DVD symbol on certain exercise pages. This is an indication of which exercises are included on the DVD.

Best of all, strength ball exercises are fun to do because of the constant challenge. It is not only about lifting more weight. It is also about having fun exploring how to coordinate more complex exercise variations. As you become more experienced with the exercises as we present them to you, you will find there are endless variations that could easily triple the size of this book. The constant challenge will motivate you to adhere to your program, and athletes and fitness participants will respond very positively. Take advantage of this powerful tool and get to the core of the matter with *Strength Ball Training*!

Exercise Finder

Exercise	Stability ball	Medicine ball	Additional equipment	On DVD	Page number
CORE STABILIZATION					
Balance Push-Up	✔				46
Bridge Ball Hug	✔				40
Bridge Perturbation	✔		BOSU DSL stability ball	✔	70
Bridge T Fall-Off	✔				32
Bridge With Medicine Ball Drops	✔	✔		✔	38
Closed Kinetic Chain (CKC) Ball Hold	✔				42
Dual-Ball Survival Rollout	✔			✔	64
Floor Push-Up to Knee Pull-In	✔		All-Legs Speed Builder		30
Full-Body Multijoint Medicine Ball Pass		✔		✔	66
Jackknife	✔				26
Kneeling Medicine Ball Self-Pass and Tracking	✔	✔			77
Kneeling Hold and Clock	✔			✔	52
Kneeling Medicine Ball Catch	✔	✔			56
Kneeling Rollout	✔				60
Lateral-Jump Ball Hold	✔			✔	44
McGill Side Raise With Static Hip Adduction	✔			✔	34
Medicine Ball Balance Catch		✔	Balance boards		68
Medicine Ball Single-Leg Balance Left to Right		✔		✔	76
One-Leg Opposite-Arm Medicine Ball Pass		✔			80
Progressive Tabletop	✔				58
Prone Balance	✔				28
Prone Balance Hip Opener	✔				29

Exercise	Stability ball	Medicine ball	Additional equipment	On DVD	Page number
Reverse Balance Push-Up	✔			✔	48
Seated Humpty Dumpty	✔	✔			55
Single-Leg Medicine Ball Self-Pass and Tracking		✔			77
Squat to Supine to Sit-Up			BOSU DSL stability ball	✔	74
Standing Ball Hug	✔				41
Standing Rollout	✔				62
Step and Push Back		✔			78
Supine Bridge Ball Hold	✔	✔			72
Supine Stabilizer Scissors	✔			✔	36
Up Up, Down Down	✔			✔	50
CORE ROTATION					
Back-to-Back 180-Degree Rotation Pass		✔			102
Back-to-Back Stop-and-Go		✔		✔	88
Goldy's Static Lateral Helicopter	✔			✔	96
Medicine Ball Standing Twist Against Wall		✔		✔	107
Over-the-Shoulder Throw		✔			90
Prone Twist	✔				95
Rotation to Overhead Lift			BOSU DSL stability ball		104
Russian Twist	✔				84
Side-to-Side Rotation Pass		✔			98
Standing Rotary Repeat			BOSU DSL stability ball	✔	106
Supine Bridge With Cross-Body Pass	✔	✔		✔	86
Supine Rotator Scissors	✔			✔	94
Twister		✔			92
V-Sit and Rotate		✔			100
LEGS AND HIPS					
Goldy's Leg Blaster	✔		Cable		128
Hip Extension and Knee Flexion	✔			✔	110
Hip Power Initiation	✔			✔	130

Exercise	Stability ball	Medicine ball	Additional equipment	On DVD	Page number
Medicine Ball Chest Pass		✔			172
One-Arm Dumbbell Press	✔		Dumbbells		152
Push-Up Pass		✔			177
Standing–Lying Partner Push-Up and Press	✔			✔	178
Standing Medicine Ball Press-Away		✔		✔	168
Standing Partner Stability Ball Chest Press	✔				174
Standing Two-Ball Rollout	✔				160
Supine Dumbbell Press and Fly	✔		Dumbbells	✔	156
Supine Push and Drive	✔		Dumbbells	✔	155
Walk-Out to Push-Up	✔			✔	162
SHOULDERS AND UPPER BACK					
Cross-Body Rear Delt Raise	✔		Dumbbells		182
Isodynamic Rear Delt Raise	✔		Dumbbells		183
Medicine Ball Shoulder Stability Circle		✔		✔	197
Medicine Ball Shoulder-to-Shoulder Pass		✔		✔	202
Medicine Ball Soccer Throw-In Passes		✔			204
Pike Push-Up	✔				198
Prone Front Raise Lateral Fly	✔		Dumbbells	✔	190
Prone Row External Rotation	✔		Dumbbells		180
Pullover	✔		Dumbbells		186
Reverse Tubing Fly	✔		Slastix tubing with handles	✔	184
Scapular Pull	✔		Dumbbells		201
Scapular Push-Up	✔			✔	196
Seated Rotator Cuff Pull	✔		Slastix tubing with handles		194
Shoulder Ball Slap	✔		Flat bench		200
Supine Lat Pull and Delt Raise	✔		Dumbbells	✔	188
Supine Pull-Up	✔		Power rack with barbell	✔	192
Wall-Based Shoulder Extension			BOSU DSL stability ball		206

Exercise	Stability ball	Medicine ball	Additional equipment	On DVD	Page number
ABDOMINALS, LOWER BACK, AND GLUTES					
Abdominal Side Crunch	✔				214
Adam's Medicine Ball Ab Lockout		✔		✔	212
Back Extension	✔				226
Ball Sit-Up to Medicine Ball Pass	✔	✔		✔	230
Prone Lat Pull			BOSU DSL stability ball		228
Reverse Back Extension	✔		Flat bench	✔	224
Supine Lower-Abdominal Cable Curl	✔		Cable with ankle strap	✔	216
Supine Lower-Abdominal Curl and Crunch	✔			✔	218
Supine Resisted Pull-In	✔				222
V-Sit Medicine Ball Transfer		✔			220
Wrap Sit-Up	✔				210
BICEPS, TRICEPS, AND FOREARMS					
Eccentric Accentuated Biceps Curl	✔		Dumbbells	✔	233
Incline Triceps Extension	✔		Dumbbells		236
Medicine Ball Push-Up		✔			238
Medicine Ball Quick Drop and Catch		✔			242
Medicine Ball Walk-Over	✔			✔	240
Overhead Medicine Ball Wall Bounce		✔			234
Standing Biceps Curl	✔		Dumbbells		232
Triceps Blaster	✔			✔	237
Wrist Curl and Extension	✔		Cable or dumbbells		239
WHOLE BODY					
Angle Lunge With Horizontal Medicine Ball Rotation		✔		✔	252
Ax Chop With Hip Flexion		✔		✔	260
Medicine Ball Circuit		✔			258
Medicine Ball Lateral to Front Overhead Throw to Wall		✔			256
Medicine Ball Overhead Jump and Throw		✔			262
Medicine Ball Overhead Lateral Bounce to Floor		✔			261

Exercise	Stability ball	Medicine ball	Additional equipment	On DVD	Page number
Medicine Ball Throw Two-Leg Jump to Single-Leg Lateral Land		✔		✔	264
Medicine Ball Walking Push-Up		✔			254
Rollover Agility			BOSU DSL stability ball	✔	248
Squat to Overhead Press			BOSU DSL stability ball		246
Stabilizing Partner Leg Press	✔				244
Walking Lunge With Overhead Medicine Ball Rotation		✔		✔	250
FLEXIBILITY					
Kneeling Posterior Shoulder Stretch	✔				273
Lateral Side Stretch	✔				269
Spinal Extension	✔				268
Standing Hamstring Stretch	✔				271
Standing Lat and Pec Stretch	✔				272
Supine Hamstring Stretch	✔				270

The Strength Ball Advantage

S trength ball training involves both stability balls and medicine balls. Although the stability ball, also known as the Swiss ball, is evolving as a cutting-edge exercise modality, the use of a ball in exercise actually dates back to the second century AD. "Exercising with a ball can stir the enthusiast or the slacker, it can exercise the lower portions of the body or the upper, some particular part rather than the whole, or it can exercise all the parts of the body equally," explained a Greek philosopher and physician. Most important, he added, "The best athletics of all are those that not only exercise the body but are able to please the spirit" (Posner-Mayer 1995).

Today's stability ball was developed in the early 1960s as a toy for children. It was adopted by physiotherapists as a means of improving patients' proprioception and balance (Posner-Mayer 1995). Several physiological mechanisms receive positive results from stability ball training. Strength and conditioning professionals and personal trainers often use stability balls in their programs. This section provides a review of the physiological mechanisms involved in stability ball training.

The human body is an amazing machine, with many sensory capabilities that allow it to carry out proper motor function. These sensory capabilities all fall under the term *proprioception*. Proprioception involves the sensation of joint movement and joint position (Lephart, Swanik, and Boonriong 1998). It contributes to the motor programming for neuromuscular control required for precise movements and contributes to muscle reflex, providing dynamic joint stability (McGill 1998).

Excellent proprioceptive capabilities are evident when an athlete has the ability to absorb a hit on the ice or playing field and maintain balance as a result of the firing of the required muscles at the optimal time, in the correct order, with an appropriate level of force. For this to occur, several physiological events occur inside the muscle. Receptors are all over the body—in the skin, tendons, and muscles—and will react when they sense a change to the tissue. This change is computed by the central nervous system and, after the brain decides how to react, the proper signals are sent to the muscles via the spinal cord and nerves for muscle contraction and hence movement.

Specific muscles of the body have more sensory capabilities than others. The rotator and intertransversarii muscles, for example, are very small segmental muscles in the spine. They cannot produce a high level of force but are very efficient at sensing vertebral position, because they have an abundance of muscle spindles. Muscle spindles are sensitive to length and rate of stretch and will cause a muscle contraction when their threshold is reached. The rotator and intertransversarii muscles, because of their minimal cross-sectional area, act as position transducers for each lumbar joint to enable the motor control system to control overall lumbar posture and avoid injury (McGill 1998). This is important in the spine and other articular structures during extreme ranges of motion, because these muscles and neighboring ligaments provide neurological feedback that directly mediates reflex stabilization in the muscles around the joint (Lephart et al. 1997). For instance, all the segmental muscles must contract to help stabilize the spine during movement. This movement may be the result of performing something consciously, or it may be unconscious as the result of a hit on the playing field or a sudden change in ground under the feet while running trails. As you will learn, strength ball training will help the body's unconscious reactions that produce appropriate movement, which often means the difference between regaining control and balance and suffering a sport injury.

Muscle spindles are the mechanisms that mediate the response from plyometric exercise. As the main stretch receptor in the muscles, when it is stretched at a particular rate and length, the muscle spindle will detect the change, send a signal to the spinal cord, and receive a message directly back that will initiate a reflex contraction in the muscle, resulting in a powerful concentric muscle contraction (Chu 1992). This is known as the myotatic stretch reflex. Here's how it works: Your extrafusal (EF) muscle fibers contract or elongate to produce movement. You also have intrafusal (IF) muscle fibers that run parallel to the EF fibers, where they are well positioned to report on the magnitude and rate of muscle lengthening and tension. When the EF fibers quickly elongate, the IF fibers stretch along with them and send a message to the spinal cord to inhibit the agonist and powerfully contract the stretched muscle. It produces this result with an extremely quick turnaround time because the message travels directly to the spinal cord and back, without having to take the longer journey up to the brain.

Golgi tendon organs (GTOs) are another type of receptor found in the body. More specifically, they are found in the musculotendinous junction. The GTO is attached end to end with extrafusal muscle fibers so it can monitor and respond to tension in a muscle and its tendon. If they reach their threshold, they will send an inhibitory signal that will result in the muscle's relaxing and shutting down. This is a protective mechanism that is used by the body under very heavy loads. A novice weightlifter, for example, would have a very low threshold, because his body has not fully adapted to the intramuscular and neuromuscular benefits of weight training. An advanced lifter, through proper training, would have a much higher threshold level than his novice counterpart, allowing him to lift much heavier loads.

Skin receptors can enhance the deeper receptors located in the muscle. Receptors in the skin of the wrist and fingers can provide information on wrist and finger movements (Lephart, Swanik, and Boonriong 1998). Visual and auditory sensors also play a part in the body's ability to function. The ability to see an oncoming hit or to hear a warning cue from a teammate allows the body to prepare itself for action. This may be in the form of muscle contraction and body segment stabilization for a change in direction to absorb the hit efficiently or make the play. A hockey player carrying the puck down the ice with his head down is vulnerable to a crushing open-ice hit. As his teammate yells, "Heads up," he will instinctively tense up, look around, and prepare his body for a hit.

Information Pathways

All information described previously is translated for the central nervous system (CNS) by not one specific receptor, but many. The coordinated efforts of all these mechanisms allow the body to meet the challenge of functional movement in a changing environment.

The receptors send their signals via afferent pathways to the CNS. There it is broken down and sent to a motor control center, where a decision will be made with regard to the mechanism of muscle contraction. The resulting muscle contraction comes about through efferent motor pathways. There, neural information is transformed into physical energy (Lephart, Swanik, and Boonriong 1998). This whole mechanism is a complex phenomenon beyond the scope of this book. The premise is illustrated in figure 1.1.

Addressing deficiencies in the neuromuscular systems, as described previously, has been a goal of therapists for many years. Lephart and colleagues (1997) believe that training to enhance joint muscle receptors should be used early in a rehabilitation protocol. Activities should focus on sudden alterations in joint positioning that necessitate reflex neuromuscular control. Additionally, some researchers have discovered that there appears to be a better recruitment pattern when the focus on training initially is one of instability and balance followed by strength training. The initial sequencing of progressions should be the introduction of unstable exercise combined with and followed by strength training. From a recruitment standpoint, the activation of antagonists and synergistic

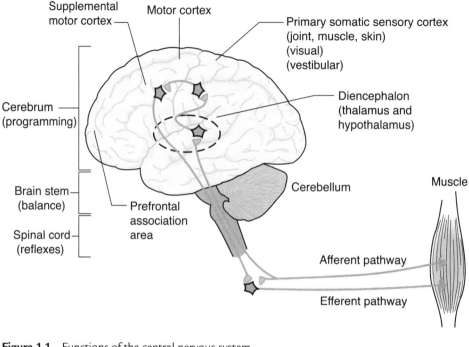

Figure 1.1 Functions of the central nervous system.

muscles will enhance muscle activation (Anderson and Behm 2005). This can be achieved through balance and postural activities. We have implemented this with our injured athletes to help them recover their athleticism and to prevent reinjury when reentering their unstable competitive environment. These types of exercises are designed to stimulate muscular coactivation (Lephart et al. 1997). This will allow for greater loading tasks for the specific joint, which will result in larger strength increases, which will result in a stronger and more functional joint. This phenomenon of increased balance and stability will lead to increased functional strength. As mentioned previously, some researchers think this is an appropriate progression. Another progression that we have also used with much success is detailed in chapter 2. Its prime focus is on the preparation of the core. By performing specific strength moves for the core, in a variety of planes, using static and dynamic contractions, athletes see positive transfer to some of the more difficult unstable exercises.

Balance

Balance is a state of bodily equilibrium or the ability to maintain the center of body mass over the base of support without falling (Irrgang, Whitney, and Cox 1994). Berg (1989) defines balance in three ways: the ability to maintain a position, the ability to voluntarily move, and the ability to react to a perturbation. All of these definitions are important for sport performance as well as for general human movement, which is challenged in balance tasks every day.

In the body, muscles make up a continuous chain that attempts to overcome disturbances in the center of gravity. The chain begins in the ankle. When a challenge of balance forces the body to lean forward, the muscles in the back of the ankle, the gastrocnemius, will contract to counteract this movement to pull the body back in balance. If balance is forced backward, the anterior tibialis muscle will contract and work to pull the body back into the center of gravity.

While standing on one leg, there is an increased challenge to balance from side to side, which will be counteracted by pronation and supination of the foot at the ankle joint. In some instances the sway of the body will be too great for only the ankle to counteract the balance challenge. When this occurs, the muscles in the legs, hips, and back counteract the movement. In this example of standing on one leg, breakdowns in strength and balance may be evident with lateral flexion (trunk), rotation (hips), poor posture (back), or excessive arm movement (shoulders and arms). The body will maintain or regain balance only if muscles act across all joints to hold the desired position.

Remember that the body is a linked system. Each muscle has receptors to assess its relative position in space and the body's overall balance. They will communicate with each other, sharing information to produce the required movement, since they all have an equally vested interest in performing well and remaining injury free.

Biomechanics and the Body

The biomechanics of movement—both in sport and everyday life—require not only strong abdominals but a strong and balanced "speed center." We identify the abdominals plus the low back, hip flexors and extensors, adductors and abductors, hip rotators, and glutes as the speed center. This name was chosen because in sport, those muscle groups initiate, assist, and stabilize all movement (Twist 1997). A hockey shot, golf swing, football throw, rugby tackle, and tennis serve are all powered by the speed center.

We know of athletes who can bench-press 300 pounds (about 136 kilograms), but once they are in a standing position, they are easily knocked off balance. That is because they have not incorporated their speed center muscles into their strength programs. Functionally, you are only as strong as your weakest links. And the weak link can lead to serious injury.

In a study by Cholewicki and McGill (1996) that examined the mechanics of powerlifters' spines during heavy lifting, one lifter (who had incurred an injury that was documented by fluoroscope) had his lumbar segments L4-L5 reach full flexion. While this happened, the other joints were able to concurrently maintain a joint angle that prevented full flexion. The authors claimed that this occurred potentially as a result of an inappropriate sequencing of muscle forces or a temporary loss of motor control wisdom. The result of this study demonstrates that the concept of segmental stability is important in injury prevention. Segmental stability can be trained effectively with strength ball exercises.

Cholewicki's study prompted a further study (McGill 1997) that would attempt to quantify the stability of the spine through a variety of loading tasks. The results of this study indicate that the occurrence of a motor control error that results in a temporary reduction in activation to one of the intersegmental muscles could allow rotation at just a single joint to the point where passive tissues, or other tissues, become irritated or even more damaged. The risk for this is greatest when high forces are in the larger muscles and simultaneous low forces are in the small intersegmental muscles (as in a maximal-squat effort) or when all muscle forces are low, such as during a low-level effort (McGill 1997).

New Research

In 2002 when the first edition of *Strength Ball Training* was released, there was limited research on the specific benefits of training with a ball and unstable surfaces, such as wobble boards. Since 2002 there have been numerous papers written on this topic that support the notions we put forward in our first edition of *Strength Ball Training*.

One area that has received attention is the research on activation of the core musculature as well as how training the core with stable and unstable devices affects core recruitment. In a study from Memorial University in Newfoundland (Behm et al. 2005), researchers looked at how unstable and unilateral (single arm or leg) resistance exercises affect trunk musculature. They used exercises that are commonly used in resistance training programs, such as shoulder press and chest press. They evaluated single-arm and dual-arm movements on an unstable ball and on a stable bench. They also used four exercises on a stability ball that challenged the core musculature in various planes and angles. What they found was something that many ball users have been experiencing for many years: Instability generated greater activation of the lower-abdominal stabilizer muscles (27.9 percent) with the core exercises and all core stabilizers (37.7 to 54.3 percent) with the chest press. Although there was no effect of instability on the shoulder press, the unilateral shoulder press produced greater activation of the back stabilizers, and the unilateral chest press resulted in higher activation of all trunk stabilizers when compared with bilateral presses.

Regardless of stability, the superman exercise was the most effective trunk-stabilizer exercise for back-stabilizer activation, whereas the McGill side bridge was the optimal exercise for lower-abdominal muscle activation. The authors concluded that the most effective means for trunk strengthening should involve back or abdominal exercises with unstable bases. Furthermore, trunk strengthening can also occur when performing resistance exercises for the limbs, if the exercises are performed unilaterally.

At the 2005 National Strength and Conditioning Association National Convention, an abstract research project was presented. It was titled "Biomechanical Comparison of the One-Arm Standing Press and Bench Press Including Muscle Response." This study validated the benefit of using single-arm movements over bilateral arm movements and how they affected the core musculature. In comparing the bench press with the standing single-arm cable press, the authors discovered that the bench press provided greater activation of the pectoralis major and the erector spinae, but with the standing single-arm cable press the activation levels for the core musculature, including rectus abdominis and obliques, were double that produced by the standard bench press. They concluded that the bench press was better for hypertrophy and strength as a result of activation level, and the standing press was more optimal for core stability and torsional challenges and a more accurate representation of what happens to the core in a standing position (Santana 2005). This is relevant to what we prescribe in *Strength Ball Training*, particularly with regard to any movement that can be described as unilateral. For example, the one-arm dumbbell press and the balance push-up progression show how the core must work significantly harder when unilateral movement or balance is challenged.

Anderson and Behm (2005) have completed a paper titled "Impact of Instability Resistance Training on Balance and Stability." The conclusion of this paper is that the introduction of instability into an exercise increases the extent of muscle activation. But there is a cost, which appears to be force production. Although a person may not be able to exert a force at the same level as in a stable environment, there may still be benefits to be obtained by using unstable devices. The decreased balance associated with strength training on an unstable surface might force limb musculature to play a greater role in joint stability. One strong example involves a person squatting on a wobble board. During the squat, the EMG (electromyographic) levels were compared with those of a standard squat. The EMG levels for several core and leg muscles were significantly higher for the same submaximal load on the wobble board than on a stable surface. The authors believe that this may be attributed to their greater need for postural and stabilizing functions in the unstable condition (Anderson and Behm 2005).

As we have moved forward since the first edition of *Strength Ball Training*, research has somewhat caught up with practitioners. The new research that we have cited lends continued credence to what thousands of trainers and users have known for years: The strength ball can enhance your efforts in the training room!

Training With the Strength Ball

2

Integration will be the key to the success of your programs. Although you can get an excellent workout with the strength ball exercises alone, you will experience even further gains if you understand how to integrate these drills with other conventional weight training exercises.

Most strength training routines involve several exercises ranging from 6 to 10 movements. This will depend on the goal of the program, the phase of training you are in, and whether or not you are completing minicircuits within your workout. Our experience tells us that depending on your goal, when integrating strength ball work into a standard program, you can do 20 to 40 percent of your exercises with a strength ball.

Positioning Strength Ball Training in a Workout

Strength ball training is useful for all populations, as it can be easily adapted to meet a variety of needs and goals. Balls of various sizes, inflation densities, and loads; exercise variations; and the dynamic stabilizing load (DSL) and load-shifting features enable neophytes and veteran athletes alike to enjoy exercises appropriate for their skill levels. However, how, when, and how much these exercises are used can vary greatly depending on the goals and abilities of the user. Strength ball training can define the complete workout for some participants, while in other applications it is common to integrate specific strength ball exercises with other types of exercises.

Dynamic Warm-Ups

The goal of a warm-up is not to stretch, and it is not just to warm a muscle. Traditional static stretches, which involve holding stationary poses, do little to prepare a body for action. In fact, current research indicates that preceding workouts and competitions with static stretching actually leads to lower strength outputs and slower speeds. Dynamic warm-ups must wake up the mind and muscles in a way that makes muscles more compliant and responsive to the mind's commands in preparing the body to move. This mental focus sets up the muscles to be at their best for the rest of the workout.

Selecting less difficult strength ball exercises or using lighter loads is suitable for preexercise, prepractice, and pregame warm-up. The low-impact, smooth weight-loaded activity takes muscles through dynamic ranges of motion, increases the temperature deep in the muscles to make them more pliable, and stimulates production of synovial fluid to lubricate joints. The instability promotes whole-body coordination, and the weighted medicine ball at the end of the body's levers activates both the muscles and the nervous system.

To begin your warm-up you should consider an activity that will increase blood flow throughout the body, which will result in an increase in core temperature. This would require six to eight minutes of light cycling, jogging, skipping rope, or exercising on a cardiorespiratory training machine. Once you complete the initial warm-up, you would progress to using some strength ball exercises for a more specific dynamic warm-up that progressively prepares the core musculature, legs, and arms for movement, balance, and force production.

Complete Functional Strength Workouts

General fitness participants can select exercises from each chapter to create a full-body workout stressing all parts of the body in roles of prime movers and stabilizers. This would significantly upgrade the workout experience for those accustomed to using selectorized weight stack machines that require little thought, focus, or coordination. The challenge of recruiting the entire body to perform an exercise will help link the kinetic chain in order to develop smarter muscles that better communicate with the rest of the body. Integrating instability and reactivity as well as the demand of using multiple muscle groups heightens the metabolic cost, expending more calories. The slow, smooth exercise execution has a mental focus and fluidity of movement similar to that of yoga.

Adult fitness enthusiasts would do well to alternate body parts, which allows them to circuit through a sequence of exercises with minimal rest to maintain an elevated heart rate. We do, however, encourage everyone to participate in other aerobic activities, such as jogging or swimming, and also integrate periods of anaerobic effort, such as hiking or cycling uphill.

Workouts for Young Athletes

When learning how to integrate strength ball training into an exercise program, you have various considerations depending on the user. Not everyone is an adult fitness participant. Young kids cannot be treated as miniature adults. They all go through various phases of growth and maturation, which require specific types of training. As kids age, they grow taller and then later fill out, adding more muscle mass. But before their bones lengthen at a fast rate, their nervous systems develop. Prepubescent children (younger than 12 years) go through a phase of peak maturation of the nervous system. This is a stage in which their coordination, body awareness, and athleticism can be improved by training with complex exercises, during which they must solve the puzzle of coordinating each exercise. Of course, training with balls is playlike and well received by children.

Children aged 8 to 12 can complete one exercise for each body part and three or four core stability exercises to begin to build strength through interesting activity that improves their neural networks. You can give kids aged 7 and younger minimal direction while turning three or four exercises into fun game challenges. Make sure the room is safe: Make sure the area is carpeted or padded, and clear the surrounding area of clutter for safe exits from the ball's surface. Then just let the kids have fun and find their own way around the ball. Most home users and gyms have 65- or 55-centimeter balls. Prepubescent children fit better on a 45-centimeter ball that accommodates their height and allows them to use the ball constructively. Young children should avoid weighted medicine ball throws until they have the core and posterior chain strength to safely handle catches, as well as the emotional maturity to pay attention to the structure needed when throwing and catching weighted balls.

Pubescent-aged kids going through a peak skeletal growth phase, typically a period of awkward growth, can use strength ball training as a complete workout to help them become accustomed to their new height and weight and regain coordination. The low-impact nature of strength ball training frees kids from other high-impact training and activities that commonly cause injury during puberty when bone levers have elongated but muscles have not grown in length, size, and strength.

Postpubescent kids have the circulating hormones to capitalize on anaerobic and weight-loaded strength training, which stimulates adaptations in muscle growth. At this stage of growth and development, strength ball training becomes a *part* of their workout as they also engage in lifts with heavier free weights.

Childhood obesity is a growing challenge . . . make that an epidemic. Overweight kids need calorie-burning and health-promoting activity, but it must be a fun and positive experience or they will be turned off. Obese children often have less coordination and are more challenged by movement. They can do better by using selectorized weight stack machines, the one activity in which they might outperform average-sized peers. Weight stack machines require little coordination, but they make strength development safer and more achievable for obese children. If the children have success, they might continue. After initial improvement, add in a small volume of simple strength ball exercises to improve their coordination and help them move more skillfully. Strength ball exercises produce higher heart rates and activate more muscles, thus causing an expenditure of calories. Therefore, it helps people win the battle of calories in versus calories out.

Sport Conditioning

Athletes of all abilities, from recreational to professional, need to train all the pillars of sport performance: strength, speed, agility, power, reaction time, and conditioning. The pillars provide the foundation for pure athleticism. With a strong foundation, a developing athlete will realize more efficient gains in his or her development. These gains, like the solid foundation of a house, will provide the basis for continual improvement.

To build strength and power and to increase the size of muscles, athletes need to use heavy loads. Depending on the athlete's training history, there could be some debate about when and how much heavy lifting is necessary. The use of heavy loads is a common practice for many athletes. In fact, one question you hear often in a strength training room filled with athletes is "How much can you squat or bench-press?" This kind of competitiveness promotes the use of heavy weights to improve performance in the bench press and squat, and it is probably one reason why we see so many overuse injuries in strength athletes.

We believe that heavy lifting too often has very little effect on athletic performance, but it is the reality when you have a group of competitive athletes training together. The squat and bench press are two of the more widely used tests for evaluating maximum strength in athletes; hence their popularity as a regular exercise. The important point is that not only is maximum strength critical to performance, but balance and coordination also play a significant role. These two components are part of linked-system strength. This concept emphasizes how the body is linked together via fascia and connective tissue and how movements that are static, such as the bench press, provide very little carryover to sport performance and do not train the body's linked system. An exercise such as a single-arm dumbbell press on a stability ball would require the use of the pectoralis major (the prime mover) as well as all the core musculature to maintain a solid positioning on the ball. It also requires the use of the glutes and hamstrings to maintain contact with the floor.

When we are in coaching mode with our athletes, we do not think about maximum strength in the classic sense (that is, bench press or squat). We recognize its importance, but we have the perspective of the body as a linked system. The components of linked-system strength as it relates to maximum strength can be enhanced through the use of the many strength ball drills in this book.

Athletes must also train speed, agility, quickness, whole-body reaction skills, and anaerobic capacity. For athletes, strength ball exercises are selected and incorporated in their overall lifting program. Sport conditioning programs would use a high volume of core stability and core rotation exercises and a smaller volume of upper-body and leg exercises that complement strength training with Olympic bars and dumbbells.

Bigger, Stronger . . . and Smarter

Bodybuilders and people who strength train recreationally who have goals of increased muscle size and better appearance can use strength ball exercises to better connect the kinetic chain and improve communication of muscles and joints to help them perform better in heavy lifts. Strength ball training can help them crash through strength plateaus by improving the neural pathways so they can use the software (brain and nervous system) as well as the hardware (bigger muscles) to drive the body to top performance.

Those who use heavy strength training programs can use a strength ball exercise that integrates balance and secures high muscle activity to potentiate muscle right before a heavy, stable lift. They might also position a strength ball exercise immediately after a heavy stable lift to work on muscle coordination under fatigue.

Rehabilitation

Rehabilitating an injury is not just about letting nature do its job. Rest time is indeed needed for a muscle or ligament to repair. But along the way, a return to action is faster and more successful with less risk of being injured again if patients participate in a well-structured strength and movement program. An injured body can use strength ball exercises to rebuild damaged areas as well as recondition close-to-healed bodies so they return to action even better than before. Return-to-play exercises must be functional to ensure the injured area is ready to handle real-life action and sport action, not just walking and sitting.

Those using rehabilitative exercises need to reeducate the body to avoid a pattern of dysfunction, in which the body compensates to cover for an injury. For example, with an injury to the left knee, the right side of the body takes on more of the body mass. There is a short-term shifting of responsibility in the body, but this can cause problems in other areas of the body. Left unchecked, these new problem areas lead to further dysfunction and injury. The bottom line is that exercises must not only tackle the initial injury but also strive to tune up and attend to the rest of the body, which was also affected by the initial injury. The process of recovery from acute injury should be directed by a medical professional who is well versed in the mechanics of exercise. This is often not a doctor but a physiotherapist or athletic therapist. Be active in the communication—take your book to the medical professional to double-check what exercises can contribute to the process at that stage. The specialist may prompt you to focus on firing specific muscles during an exercise and make other meticulous adjustments that require professional guidance.

Initial injury is often caused by other problems in the body. We speak to treating the cause, not the symptom, and often an injury is caused by other weak links in the chain that, over time, cause a seemingly unrelated injury. If you have had an injury, chances are your body still needs to be corrected and tuned up. Many people exist with minor pain and strength imbalances that negatively affect their ability to perform at their best in activities and leave them at risk of further injury.

Whole-body reeducation includes smooth, whole-body strength exercises that fire muscles in the correct sequence and stimulate the proprioceptive system to repair software and muscles together. Strength ball exercises draw on multiple body parts to get the job done properly, forcing the body to work together and expose weak links in the kinetic chain. If strength ball exercise does not help correct patterns of dysfunction, try an easier version with the goal of laying a proper foundation in the body. If a weak link or any discomfort persists, we encourage you to refer to a medical professional who specializes in injury assessment and active, exercise-based rehabilitation. It is important for professionals such as personal trainers and coaches to stay within their scope of practice and refer clients to a team of professionals—chiropractors, physiotherapists, massage therapists, acupuncture, and so on—to the benefit of the client. Likewise, to link your exercise and sport goals to the process, you should select a medical professional who is competent and current in exercise application and knowledgeable about the demands of sport. For the home user, level-appropriate strength ball training will help build from the center of the body out and link the kinetic chain together. If you have a new injury or an old minor problem that persists, we recommend that you get the short-term advice of exercise and medical professionals who can give you hands-on assessment and map out your precise program.

Workouts During Travel

A deflated and folded stability ball is an excellent training tool to take on the road. It travels easily, and upon inflation, it can be used in hotel rooms, at cottages, and in other locations. Many business people who travel frequently pack a ball and accompanying exercise book, using a hotel room for a quick and convenient workout. Strength ball training helps combat the fatigue of travel, helps reset the body's clock when changing time zones, and keeps you on a consistent schedule in your workouts. Given enough time, it is fairly easy to go for a short run or climb some hotel stairs for aerobic conditioning. Adding a whole-body strength ball routine keeps you progressing instead of falling behind on strength and function. Business travelers who do not feel safe running in an unfamiliar city can circuit through several strength ball exercises in their hotel rooms, at a work rate that sustains an elevated heart rate to achieve fitness for the heart and lungs. Some travelers do carry two- or four-pound medicine balls (1 to 2 kilograms) for self-tracking exercises. This works great with checked luggage. For carry-on luggage only, we recommend a stability ball and Slastix strength tubing with a door attachment, which is much lighter than weighted medicine balls.

Strength Ball Use in the Workplace

Most jobs have repetitive tasks, such as working on an assembly line or sitting at a desk typing and talking on the phone. Having access to strength balls allows for short active breaks to stretch and actively strengthen muscles and balance the body. A couple of short exercise breaks over the long term can improve strength, balance, and fitness. In the short term, an exercise break with an unstable ball activates all the muscles in the body, not just those used in the workplace, and recharges the body and mind. Taking a break from workplace tasks to awaken the mind and body can improve your work performance and prevent repetitive-use injuries. People in office settings can develop poor posture as they slouch over their computer keyboards. Active sitting on a stability ball helps maintain good posture and quietly works on core stability, engaging all of the postural muscles. People in office settings often select black stability balls, which are much more corporate in appearance than brighter-colored balls.

Choosing Exercises and Progressions

When starting any new fitness program, begin at a level that will reinforce proper technique and movement patterns. This is especially important with strength ball training, which also challenges stability. Once you have mastered a particular move, then you should continually challenge yourself with the appropriate exercise progressions to ensure success in your program.

Selecting Exercises

To get you started, we recommend you include exercises from all chapters. We prefer to build from the center of the body out, preferentially training the core first and then the periphery (arms and legs). In many weight room workouts, we may prescribe more sets for core than we do for other muscle groups. However, *all* of the exercises in this book feature good core activation, so an equal representation from all chapters works well because all exercises involve the core. However, to keep primary core exercise safe, work on abdominal and core stability exercises for several weeks as a foundation before training core rotation.

Remember that before even beginning strength ball training, and if you are new to strength training in general, you should develop some base-level strength with stability training, as described under the heading Precautions on page 21 of this chapter. Once you are ready to begin strength ball training, note that the exercises in each chapter are listed in order from easiest to most difficult. This ranking is determined by the intensity of the physical exertion required as well as the complexity of the coordination needed for successful completion of the exercise. Skipping ahead will only cause your body to compensate and cheat to get an exercise done, setting you up for injury. Take your time and practice a group of exercises before progressing to new exercises of greater difficulty.

Keep in mind that within each exercise are tips on regressing to make an exercise easier and progressing an exercise to make it more challenging. Regressions are often applied on the spot, when you try an exercise and find it too difficult. A quick adjustment can make it more achievable. Progressions are often applied toward planning the *next* workout after you notice certain exercises have become easier to complete. Each workout should be a challenge to you. If you have achieved your repetition goal, you should consider a slight increase in your medicine ball weight, the addition of two or three repetitions per set, or an adjustment to the body mechanics to make the exercise more challenging. Specific methods to increase the difficulty of an exercise are listed for each exercise. General rules for progressing an exercise are listed in the following sections. A keen understanding of those rules will help you refine your workout to the precise difficulty level each time—not too easy, not resulting in mechanical breakdown, but challenging enough to produce the best results.

Stability Ball Progressions

There are numerous methods of progressing the level of difficulty when using stability ball exercises. Specific structured progressions are documented in the text of each exercise. But knowing several guidelines to simplify or advance an exercise will allow you to modify each exercise many times over to define the most appropriate level of challenge for you. If you are uncertain, you should choose regressions to ensure that you complete the exercise safely within your current abilities. However, when you are experienced with an exercise and begin to find it easy, adopt progressions to make sure you are challenged. If an exercise is not challenging, you will not stimulate improvement. With this in mind, the following are points that you can consider when regressing or progressing your exercises.

• **Change the base of support.** By decreasing the base of support for an exercise, you can increase the challenge of balance. You can accomplish this by increasing the inflation of the ball, which will result in a smaller base of ball support. You can also change the base of support by moving from a four-point support to a three- or two-point support. An example of a four-point support is a stability ball push-up in which you have both hands on the ball and both feet on the floor. To increase the level of difficulty in the push-up, you can use a three-point base of support. For example, you could raise one foot off the floor. You can also decrease your base of support by placing your hands and feet closer together. Although you are still in a four-point base of support, this move results in a decreased overall base of support.

• **Change the length of the lever.** As you alter the length of your lever arm from short to long, you increase the difficulty of the exercise, as with the abdominal crunch medicine ball throw. Throwing from the chest is easier than using a longer lever and throwing from overhead. Your trunk can also be the lever arm between the floor and ball contacts. A short rollout is easier than a longer rollout. A short ball bridge is easier than a longer one. Minor changes in body position can make a dramatic difference in level of difficulty by changing the coordination, effort, or force required.

• **Increase range of motion.** By increasing movements from a smaller to a larger range of motion, you can increase the difficulty of the exercise, as with the push-up with hands on ball. You can progress from partial push-ups to full-range push-ups.

- **Change the speed of movement.** Changing the tempo of an exercise changes the result. Very slow movements keep the muscle loaded under tension longer and help build strength and stability. Fast dynamic movements tend to build power. The tempo of movement also makes the exercise easier or more difficult. Most experts suggest that moving faster is more difficult. But there is no general rule here. Some exercises done more quickly are much more difficult. Still other exercises done very slowly require much more strength and balance. Know that speed of movement alters the demands. You will need to adjust your tempo on an exercise to learn whether it results in an easier or more difficult execution.

- **Add resistance.** You can increase the intensity of an exercise by adding some form of loaded resistance, such as a medicine ball, an external free weight, cable, or elastic tubing, as with the jackknife exercise with a cable attached to the legs (see page 26). For safety, we recommend Slastix tubing made by Stroops, which is thick, strong tubing with handles covered with a protective sleeve. The Hip/ Thigh Blaster tubing (also made by Stroops) connects to the ankles and is covered with a protective sleeve. Strength tubing needs to be long enough to accommodate whole-body moves in strength ball training. It also needs to be strong enough to offer enough resistance. It should come with a protective sleeve to make the tubing more durable and, if it does eventually break, to make sure it coils inside the sleeve instead of snapping back and hitting you.

- **Close the eyes.** By closing your eyes, you increase the proprioceptive demand in the body, flooding other sensors and receptors positioned to give feedback on changes to muscle, ligaments, tendons, and joint position. Removing visual feedback overloads your proprioceptive system, forcing those "minibrains" to work harder and improve. This adds a level of difficulty, but you should take caution. Some exercises will require spotting by a strength coach, such as kneeling on the ball.

Medicine Ball Progressions

Selecting the correct medicine ball load and modifying the method of applying the medicine ball also contribute to making an exercise level appropriate.

- **Increase ball weight.** As strength and power improve, selecting a heavier medicine ball will progress the amount of overload placed on the muscles, stimulating further adaptations.

- **Introduce throwing variables.** With a ball of the same weight, increase the distance between partners. This requires more power on the throw and more coordination and eccentric strength on the catch. Or move closer together and increase the catch–throw speed. This requires reactions and eye–hand coordination and shifts the emphasis to power, training the eccentric–concentric coupling.

- **Use a single arm.** Changing from two-hand catches to single-hand catches increases the reliance on the core, hips, and legs, along with the posterior chain, to absorb the load. In general, it increases the complexity of the exercise, forcing greater whole-body involvement.

- **Use vision tracking.** For exercises with a medicine ball, locking vision on the ball as it travels increases the balance challenge. For example, stand on one leg while passing the ball overhead, or move it from one side of the body to the other. Think of tunnel vision, seeing nothing but the ball. If you also add a head tilt—tilting your head back to look up at the ball overhead—the level of balance difficulty is heightened.

- **Integrate movement or balance.** Adding movement to whole-body exercises or instability will increase the metabolic cost, coordination required, muscle activation, number of muscles recruited, and transferability.

- **Make the exercise unpredictable.** Throwing the ball at varied times or throwing the ball to different positions requires quick reactions, quick thinking, and quick body adjustments to nail the mechanics needed for a whole-body catch. For example, in partner passes, pass the ball to the right, left, up high, down low, and overhead. Mixing it up is fun and makes the muscles more responsive.

Selecting Training Tools

Stability balls can now be found in just about any type of store—department stores, supermarkets, and even drug stores. With so many options and choices of balls, how can you determine which one might be appropriate for you? The following tells you everything you need to know.

Sizing of Stability Balls

Most manufacturers of stability balls make sizing recommendations based on your height. One general rule that has been stated is that when you sit on the ball, your thighs should be parallel to the floor. If they are below the parallel level, you will be forced to use poor posture for many of the exercises. In many cases, this rule is a good general guideline to use when determining your ball size. But as you will see in the exercise descriptions, this rule does not always hold true. Many exercises use a number of ball sizes through their progressions. In your training facility you should have several different-sized balls available.

For personal use, those who are 5 feet, 10 inches to 6 feet, 3 inches (178 to 190 centimeters) can accomplish most exercises with 55-centimeter and 65-centimeter balls. Those who are 5 feet, 9 inches or shorter (175 centimeters or less) can use 45-centimeter and 55-centimeter balls. Those who are 6 feet, 4 inches or taller (193 centimeters or taller) can work with 65-centimeter and 75-centimeter balls.

Quality of Stability Balls

Stability balls have become a more common training tool in the mainstream populations, and mass merchandisers now stock the product on a regular basis. With many more options than in the past, shoppers are able to choose from bargain-basement balls at general retailers to specialty balls off the Internet. We encourage you to shop for quality. This is a tool that must support your body weight and handle the rigors of physical training. If the ball looks and feels on the thin side, like a beach ball, you can assume it is a cheaper product. If it feels thicker, it might be of good quality.

The accurate measure is in the ABS rating. Stability balls are labeled ABS if they are truly an "antiburst" ball. When a ball is punctured, ABS balls will slowly deflate instead of bursting immediately. Balls that are lab tested are assigned a weight they can handle and still demonstrate reliable antiburst properties. Look for a ball with an ABS rating for 300 pounds (136 kilograms) or more. Balls are also tested for the total amount of weight they can support. This is usually about three times their ABS rating. A 300-pound ABS ball could hold 900 pounds (408 kilograms). For more information on stability balls, you can search online at www.athleteconditioning.com or check out a specialty fitness retailer.

BOSU Dynamic Stabilizing Load (DSL) Balls

BOSU is an acronym for both sides up. DSL stands for dynamic stabilizing load. The BOSU DSL stability ball was invented by David Weck, creator of the BOSU Balance Trainer. Weck's training tools allow coaches and exercise practitioners to create new exercises. The dynamic stabilizing load inside the ball is a granular substance that provides stability when the ball sits on the floor, a load to lift when the ball is carried off the floor, and a perturbation when the DSL shifts from side to side.

When the ball is on the floor, the load inside the DSL stability ball makes the ball slightly more stable, aiding in mastery of new exercises and making them safer. DSL stability balls come with 5 pounds (about 2.3 kilograms) of load inside the ball. To increase the stabilizing factor, which could be important in rehabilitation settings and with aging clients, you can add sand to increase the load inside the ball. The increased ground-based stability allows the ball to be used by many people who could not otherwise use a regular stability ball, yet it still provides an unstable surface and light instability on the floor. For advanced exercisers who lift heavy dumbbells, the load keeps the ball in place, providing a reliable target to sit on with dumbbells in hand.

Exercisers incur an additional demand when lifting the ball off the floor. Stabilizer muscles are targeted during exercises in which the ball is against the wall, which requires a more active contraction not only to hold the ball in place or roll the ball but also to press in firmly against the ball.

The dynamic stabilizing load inside the ball provides audible feedback during movement drills. If controlled, fluid movement is the objective, the load should remain resting at the bottom of the ball, making no sound. Strong or fast shifts in the ball—such as from side to side across the body—are similar to the action of throwing water out of a bucket, except you get to brake and stop the "water." This requires excellent core bracing and effective muscle contractions in the back, shoulders, and arms. Rapid shifts back and forth over a shorter range of motion impose perturbations that increase muscle activation around joints. You will learn to judge the strength of the shift and the abruptness of the braking by the tempo and volume of the shifting DSL. For more information, refer to www.athleteconditioning.com.

Options in Medicine Balls

Similar to dumbbells, medicine balls come in various weights. Most women and kids will handle a 4-, 6-, or 8-pound ball (about 2, 3, and 4 kilograms, respectively). Men most often select an 8- or 10-pound ball (about 4 or 5 kilograms). For some exercises, elite athletes use 25- and 30-pound balls (about 12 and 14 kilograms, respectively). (Note that these metric conversions for ball weights are not precise. That is, a 2-kilogram ball is actually 4.4 pounds. Some brands of medicine balls are available in metric weights only, and some are available in English weights only.) Try some exercises in the gym or with your personal trainer to get a better idea of the weight range best suited to your strength level. Having at least two medicine balls, one of medium and one of heavy weight, will accommodate a large number of exercises. Once you have a set weight to work with, there are several ways to make a drill more difficult, even with a ball of the same weight.

Several kinds of medicine balls are available. They all produce the dynamic load required for building strength, so make your choice based on individual preference for their other features. Original medicine balls were big and leather bound. You can also select rubber medicine balls that are slightly smaller than a basketball. PowerBounce medicine balls are constructed of thick rubber, are virtually indestructible, and they bounce off the floor or wall. Today many people opt for soft-shell fitness balls. They are small and soft, so they can be gripped in one hand. They're also great for tracking exercises. Some people find them softer to catch. For more information on medicine balls go to www.athleteconditioning. com or check out a specialty fitness retailer.

Technique Notes

As strength and conditioning coaches, we have more than 30 combined years of experience in working with professional athletes and more than 50 combined years of experience in fitness. Enforcing proper technique has been the foundation of our success. Do not settle for anything less when you are training yourself or your clients. A component that is common to every exercise in *Strength Ball Training* is the concept of setting the core. You will achieve greater levels of stability and strength if you can master this technique and use it as you train yourself or coach your clients.

Setting the Abdominals

Since the first edition of *Strength Ball Training* there has been much debate about the optimal method of setting the core to provide a solid pillar for completing exercise movements. The following statement appeared in the first edition of this book: Setting the abdominals is a simple, yet important, technique in the setup phase of all stability ball and medicine ball exercises. Slightly drawing in your navel toward your spine and giving your pelvis an anterior tilt (which emphasizes the natural curve in your lower back) accomplishes the setting of the abdominals. This drawing in serves a significant function. Most important, it initiates a support mechanism for the spine and torso as a result of the transverse abdominis and internal obliques muscles being activated. This motion of drawing in has been demonstrated to assist in the reduction of compression on the spine by as much as 40 percent, as well as promoting the natural function of these muscles. When this contraction is activated, it provides your body with a much more stable core area for executing all exercises (Richardson et al. 1999; Wirhed 1990).

In Stuart McGill's book *Low Back Disorders* (2002), he emphasizes a technique known as bracing, which is an isometric contraction that results in coactivation of the obliques and transverse abdominis. McGill states that this method provides increased stability, and it more readily prepares the body for unexpected loads. He also claims that it provides for a greater base of pull for muscles than the hollowing, or drawing-in, technique, which decreases the base. It has been our experience that a combination of the two techniques brings about a more solid core. This would involve a slight hollowing of the abdominals along with a slight isometric contraction.

We cue our athletes to contract 360 degrees around the core to set the core. With younger kids, to help them achieve the sensation of bracing, we have fun faking a punch to the belly—at which they instinctively brace. It is a simple way to establish the isometric contraction. For older clients, we make the analogy of a corset so that they sense a stabilized trunk before each exercise. Whatever the cue, a blend of drawing in and bracing sets the core to absorb and produce loadings and to provide a better base from which the arms and legs can generate force. With training, this will become natural. After weeks of strength ball training, you will notice that you begin to automatically set the core for tasks outside the gym, such as reaching to lift a heavy object off a shelf or skiing on very difficult mogul runs. Enjoy your results applied during day-to-day tasks and in your favorite sport!

Precautions

One of the issues that we have seen since the release of the first edition of *Strength Ball Training* is a misuse of some exercise progressions. As good as the ball looks for increasing core strength and stability, there are instances in which it should not be used. Two of these instances are in people with chronic low back pain and those who are just beginning a strengthening program. These recommendations are grounded in the fact that increased activation of the core musculature also involves an increase in spinal loads. That is not necessarily a bad thing, but proper progression will ultimately insure against any kind of injury. It has been suggested that the proper progression would involve the use of stable surfaces and then progress to unstable surfaces (McGill 2002). Introduction of unstable surfaces such as stability balls should only be done once you or your client has sufficient spinal stability to be able to accept loads that will challenge the core without pain during and after the exercise. You may want to spend three to eight weeks doing exercises on stable surfaces before progressing to the greater challenge of stability ball training.

The following are a few stable exercises that we recommend if you are beginning a program. You should be able to do these exercises comfortably before progressing to the more advanced unstable exercises.

Figure 2.1 demonstrates the static back extension. Hold the body in perfect alignment so that there is a line from the ear to the shoulder, hips, and knee. There should be a very slight bend in the knee during this exercise. Do not allow the knees to hyperextend, which can place undue stress on the backs of the knees. Your goal for this exercise is to hold the position for two to three minutes. Do not start your program by attempting to complete long sets. Begin with sets of 30 seconds and slowly progress weekly by adding 10 to 15 seconds to each set.

Figure 2.1   Static back extension.

Figure 2.2 shows the McGill static side raise, also known as the static side plank. McGill has done much research on spinal biomechanics. Again, as you can see in the setup, there should be a fairly straight line from the head all the way down to the feet. You may find it too difficult to begin this move from the feet. If so, try flexing the knees to 90 degrees and eventually progress to straight legs. Your goal for this will be to hold the position for 90 to 120 seconds. Begin with sets of 30 seconds and slowly progress weekly by adding 10 to 15 seconds to each set.

Figure 2.3 shows the single-leg hip lift. While lying on your back, flex at one hip and hold this position with your arms. The opposite knee should be flexed so that your foot is flat on the floor. Set your core and press your foot into the floor to raise your hips off the floor. Press up to a point where you have a line from your knee to the hip to the shoulder. Your goal for this movement is to be able to complete at least 10 repetitions on each side with good form.

Figure 2.2 McGill static side raise.

Figure 2.3 Single-leg hip lift.

If you want to train your core while focusing on other body parts, you should consider exercises that focus on using single-arm movements.

For athletes preparing for high-force dynamic movement and for fitness enthusiasts who strength-train, the intersegmental and stabilizing muscles must be well developed to prevent injury. These intersegmental and stabilizing muscles in the spine, shoulders, hips, knees, and ankles can best be stimulated and overloaded by performing exercises in an unstable environment. The stability ball provides this very environment, which will give you several viable options to enhance your exercise toolkit.

Common Terms

As you use the exercises in this book, you will encounter some common terms that describe positions or movements. These include the following:

Tabletop, or bridge, is the act of lying on the ball with your head and shoulders supported, your feet under your knees, and your core engaged. In this position you will resemble a tabletop or bridge.

Supine involves lying on the back or with your face upward. When you lie on your bed on your back you are in a supine position.

Prone involves lying on your front or facing the floor. When you lie on your bed on your belly, you are in a prone position.

Static means no movement. So an exercise requiring a static hold would result in the contraction of muscles with no movement being produced.

Throughout the book you will see numbers designating **tempo**, such as "1:1:1 tempo." Each digit of the number represents a phase of the movement. In this example, there are three phases, and each phase is to be held for one second. Generally the first number represents the lowering, or the eccentric portion of the lift. The middle number represents the middle position of the range of motion, and the final number is the speed of the concentric portion, or the raising of the weight.

The fundamental concepts that we have covered in this chapter may seem elementary, but in essence they are critical to your success in executing the exercises described in the book. These foundational concepts will lead you down the path of success with your programming.

Core Stabilization

Exercises in This Chapter

To shift the load to your lower abdominals and hip flexors, add this exercise to your program. It requires upper-body and core stability and activates the lower abs and hip muscles to draw the ball in toward the body. The weight in your lower body is transferred through the ball to produce a load against the hip flexors.

Setup

Standing behind the ball, crouch down and place your abdomen on top of the ball. Roll forward until your hands reach the floor in front of the ball. Walk your hands out until only your feet remain on top of the ball. Contract the core to hold a strong link. Your body should be in a straight and firm line from feet to head.

Movement

From the prone push-up position, keep the legs straight and bend at the waist so the hips elevate and the knees move closer to the torso. This moves the ball toward your hands. Keep the speed of movement under control, with a 1:1:1 tempo.

Finish

Extend your legs to move the ball back to the start position. At this point, at the end of each rep, your body should be linked with strong contractions forming one level, straight line.

Tips and Progressions

- One method of progression is to add resistance to the ankles. You can accomplish this by adding a cable or strength tubing. So as you flex your hips forward, you are not only pulling on the ball but also the resistance of the cable.
- Another progression is a modified one-leg, bent-knee jackknife. In this version, begin with only one foot on the ball. The right leg is off the ball yet straight and firm. Draw the ball up toward your chest with your lower abdominals and hip flexors. Balance on one leg in this position, holding your contraction, before straightening the left leg back to the setup position, following a 1:2:1 tempo.

a

b

PRONE BALANCE

The prone balance is also known by some as a prone plank position. It provides a challenge to the core in the sagittal plane.

Setup

Roll out on a stability ball so that it is set under your elbows in a prone position. You should be propped up on your elbows, with your shoulders placed directly over your elbows. Engage your core to create a slight kyphotic posture (back rounded) and hold this position. Your feet should be hip-width apart.

Movement and Finish

There is no real movement for the prone balance because it is a static exercise. Hold the described position for 30 to 120 seconds.

Tips and Progressions

- You can use many progressions during this exercise. The first to consider is foot placement. Progress from a hip-width stance to a narrow stance or single-leg stance.
- Change the effective lever arm by rolling the ball forward, from side to side, in circles, and in figure eights.
- Add resistance by wearing a weight vest or placing a sandbag over the low back.
- You can achieve greater instability by placing the feet on top of a BOSU or balance board.
- Also see prone ball hold with knee drive (page 132) as a variation with some hip movement.

The prone balance hip opener is similar to the push-up position hip opener (page 124) and the prone balance. It adds the component of hip mobility to the prone balance and changes the balance challenge of the push-up position hip opener from the feet to the arms.

Setup

Roll out on a stability ball so that you are in a prone position with the ball set under your elbows. You should be propped up on your elbows with your shoulders directly over your elbows.

Movement

Flex one hip forward to create a 90-degree angle. Adduct the leg as far as you can, squeeze this position for a second, then abduct out to the side.

a

Finish

Complete a number of reps and then switch legs.

Tips and Progressions

- Increase the challenge of this movement by adding a hip extension after each hip rotation. To do this, after you have abducted the hip and returned to the start position, extend the hip straight back, hold, return to the start position, then proceed with hip adduction.
- Add resistance by putting weights on your ankle.

b

This exercise combines a stability ball with an All-Legs Speed Builder, a tool that has two lengths of strength tubing with ankle cuffs. The amount of resistance is suitable for loading the lower abdominals. When setting up for the exercise, the length of prestretch on the tubing defines the load experienced at the middle position. It works best to have at least a light prestretch on the tubing. This makes the load and movement smoother.

Setup

Begin crouched behind the stability ball, moving on top of the ball and walking out (with hands) until you are in a prone push-up position, hands on the floor, feet on top of the ball. With straight arms, use scapular retraction to set the upper back before bending the elbows. You can tell you are in the correct position if you feel your upper back loaded, not just the shoulders and arms. Contract the core to hold a stable position on the ball, keeping the hips up level with the feet and shoulders.

Movement

Complete one push-up, and then hold the arms almost straight while drawing the knees in toward the chest. As you draw the knees in toward the chest, you will feel the resistance of the Speed Builder challenging the lower abdominals. Pause before slowly extending the legs to return to the setup position.

Tips and Progressions

- You will have greater strength gains by following slow, steady movements to keep the muscles under tension for longer periods. Aim to achieve a set of 10 with a 2:2:2 speed of movement, taking 2 seconds to do the push-up phase, 2 seconds to draw the knees to the chest, and 2 seconds to extend the legs, for a total of 60 seconds.
- To deemphasize upper-body strength and focus on core strength, change the ratio of push-ups to pull-ins. For example, produce one push-up followed by three pull-ins. Or eliminate the push-up, holding the prone position and completing more pull-ins. That approach works well if you increase the amount of load you are pulling.

a

b

The bridge is a key position that dozens of exercises build from. Bridge fall-offs activate the deep abdominal muscles and all core muscles to hold the bridge, brake before falling, and pull back into position. It works 360 degrees around the torso.

Setup

Sit on top of the ball and slowly roll forward so your hips move off the ball. Continue until your middle back is on top of the ball. You will feel your shoulder blades at the top or middle of the ball. Your feet are flat on the floor and shoulder-width apart, upper legs parallel to the floor. The key to a functional bridge is to elevate your hips to form a straight line from neck to knees. Be sure to hold your hips up strong. Raise your arms out to the side so that your torso and arms make a T position.

Movement

Slowly shift your weight to one side, rolling out onto your triceps. Keep your hips up, not allowing any rotation at the hips or shoulders. Move as far to the side as you can without losing your solid position and without falling off the ball.

Finish

Using your core muscles, pull your body back across the ball until your shoulder blades are back on top of the ball. Continue to move through to the opposite side and repeat the movement.

Tips and Progressions

- Place a dowel across the chest from shoulder to shoulder to evaluate stability and body alignment. Any hip or torso rotation will be evident when the dowel rolls or tips and falls off.
- Successful execution of bridge fall-offs can lead to reaction fall-offs. When your partner lightly pushes you to the left or the right, you must react and decelerate the movement with your core muscles, reversing the movement before falling off of the ball. This is more sportlike because you are not worried as much about strict technique as you are about producing the resulting function. You will tend to roll your torso when pushed to the extreme side ranges before braking and returning to your middle setup position.

MCGILL SIDE RAISE WITH STATIC HIP ADDUCTION

 This exercise is named after Stuart McGill, one of the world's leading spine researchers, from the University of Waterloo. This movement focuses on frontal plane core musculature while incorporating the hip adductors.

Setup

Lie sideways on a mat with your elbow propping up your body. You should have your body set so you are supported laterally. Place a stability ball between your feet and squeeze to fire your adductors on your hips.

Movement

Engage your core, and laterally lift your body off the floor, maintaining the adductor contraction on the ball. There should be a fairly straight line from your ear to shoulder, hips, and knees. Hold the contracted position one to two seconds.

Finish

After holding the contracted position, lower yourself back to the starting position. As you lower your hips back down, do not allow your body to rest. At about a centimeter from the floor, begin your next lift. Repeat on the opposite side after reps are completed.

Tips and Progressions

- To work static strength and stability of your core, try static holds in the contracted position. Holds can be anywhere from 30 to 90 seconds in length on each side.
- Add extra resistance by placing a sandbag or weight vest over your hips.

SUPINE STABILIZER SCISSORS
===

 Although it has a similar name as Supine Rotator Scissors on page 94, the main difference here is that Supine Stabilizer Scissors utilizes the ball as a base of support and focuses on sagittal-plane strength.

Setup

Place a ball in front of something solid that you can grip on to—either a power rack or a solid piece of equipment. The height you have to grasp is approximately hip height. Lie back over the stability ball so it is providing support to your low back. Reach back and grasp the bar with extended arms. Your legs should also be extended and parallel with the floor.

Movement

Begin movement by raising one leg straight up and lowering the opposite leg approximately 10 to 15 degrees.

Finish

Hold this position for a second, and then reverse your legs.

Tips and Progressions

This movement provides a great challenge to the low back and abdominals from a stability standpoint. If you feel pain during this movement, it might be a result of your not having the required base strength to maintain your position. In this case, you can try the movement with bent knees.

BRIDGE WITH MEDICINE BALL DROPS

 This exercise requires the core muscles to eccentrically decelerate the falling load (medicine ball) while producing stabilization to hold the basic bridge and to balance and return to balance after catching the ball.

Setup

Sit on top of the ball and slowly roll forward so your hips move off the ball. Continue until your middle back is on top of the ball. Your shoulder blades will be at the top or middle of the ball. Your feet are flat on the floor and shoulder-width apart, and upper legs are parallel to the floor. The key to a functional bridge is to elevate your hips to form a straight line from neck to knees. Hold your hips up strong. Extend your arms up above your chest, with your hands ready in a catching position.

Movement

Your partner stands in front of you, lightly tossing a medicine ball so it drops outside of your center of gravity. You must rotate slightly and catch the ball as it drops to the right or left of your chest area. Catch the ball while keeping your hips up.

Finish

Brake, balance, and throw the ball back to your partner before using your core to return to the setup position in preparation for the next rep.

Tips and Progressions

- Randomize the medicine ball tosses from left to right, above shoulder to waist level, as well as overhead.
- Give the spotter feedback if you can handle more challenging drops.
- Likewise, the spotter needs to remind you to keep your hips up strong and bring the feet back to the starting stance. Most people automatically widen their stance when catching the ball instead of relying on their core strength.
- To increase the difficulty of the exercise, bring your feet together.

a

b

BRIDGE BALL HUG

The bridge ball hug introduces the concept of static and dynamic contractions in the same exercise.

Setup

Sit on top of the ball and slowly roll forward so your hips move off the ball. Continue until your middle back is on top of the ball. Your shoulder blades will be at the top middle of the ball. Your feet are flat on the floor and shoulder-width apart, and upper legs are parallel to the floor. The key to a functional bridge is to elevate your hips to form a straight line from neck to knees. Hold your hips up strong. Place another ball on your chest, wrapping your arms around the ball as if you were hugging the ball.

Movement

Maintain your setup position while a partner begins slapping the ball in multiple angles. The key is to hug the ball as tightly as possible and limit movement of your body and ball during the slaps. Setting your abdominals during this exercise will assist in stabilizing your body.

Finish

This exercise is finished when you complete the total number of slaps in a set; 20 to 30 slaps are recommended.

Tips and Progressions

Increase the difficulty by holding the ball away from your body with arms extended over your chest.

The standing ball hug is a progression from the bridge position. The standing position is the most sport-specific position you can be in.

Setup

Place your feet shoulder-width apart, with the hips back and shoulders forward over your knees. This is a very athletic position, the one you want to maintain for this exercise. In this position, you will hug a ball at torso level.

Movement

Your partner begins by push-slapping the ball in multiple directions as you attempt to maintain your setup position.

Finish

This exercise is finished when you complete the total number of slaps in a set; 20 to 30 slaps are recommended.

Tips and Progressions

Advance the strength demands and muscle recruitment by having your partner push harder on the ball. Use rapid-fire pushes to retain the reactivity that the ball slaps produce.

CLOSED KINETIC CHAIN (CKC) BALL HOLD

This exercise can add to or replace ball hugs; the difference is the use of an athletic stance and holding the ball away from the body. This is an essential exercise for any athlete. It builds strength and stability. Developing core stability in the closed kinetic chain is a crucial step to linking your core with posture and building the core musculature to contribute to whole-body strength and movement drills.

Setup

Get into an athletic-ready stance with your feet shoulder-width apart and your ankles, knees, and hips slightly flexed. Hold a stability ball in front of you at chest height with the arms almost fully extended and hands pressing in against the sides of the ball. Set the shoulders and middle back by pulling the shoulder blades up, back, and down so that your chest is up and out. Squeezing the stability ball will help to stabilize the shoulder blades. Do not let the stability ball touch the torso.

Movement

A training partner or coach applies strong three-second pushes, alternating directly to the left and right. Maintain a contracted core, middle back, hips, and lower body. Own your position, trying to prevent your partner from moving the ball from the starting position. Think of anchoring this position, being strong to prevent the ball from being pushed off the midline. Lock your rib cage onto your hips to prevent any rotation through the trunk or flexion and extension.

Tips and Progressions

- The push is timed at three seconds to give you time to figure out what muscles to activate to counteract the push and achieve strong muscle contractions.
- Partners should not be shy about applying force. If the exerciser shows too much rotation, ease up. If the exerciser is anchored in, add more force.
- To increase difficulty, apply more force or hold the ball farther from the body, which increases the lever length from the ball to the midline.
- You can also begin to vary the direction of push, adding diagonal and vertical push patterns.
- After a number of workouts with steady pushes, decrease the length of each push while increasing the sequence pace, applying fast repetitive strikes ("fast repeats") from various directions.
- When you are no longer challenged, progress by closing the eyes.

Lateral-jump ball hold is similar in principle to the CKC ball hold. This exercise incorporates lateral movement mechanics with CKC core stability, linking the core to lateral deceleration and balance.

Setup

You need enough space for two athletes to jump side to side. Begin by getting into an athletic-ready stance with your feet shoulder-width apart and with your ankles, knees, and hips slightly flexed. Hold the stability ball in front of you at chest height with arms almost fully extended, hands pressing in against the sides of the ball. Set the shoulders and middle back by pulling the shoulder blades up, back, and down so that your chest is up and out. Squeezing the stability ball will help to stabilize the shoulder blades. Do not let the ball touch the torso.

Movement

To begin the exercise, preload the legs and jump laterally off 2 feet (61 centimeters) to your left. Land softly and absorb the landing by engaging your core and triple-flexing your ankles, knees, and hips. Immediately upon landing, have your partner or coach apply a three-second push to the ball, pushing from the inside. Think of *land–contract–hold*. Keep your shoulders stabilized and chest up to prevent any movement to the ball and any breakdown in posture. Repeat in the opposite direction, and alternate jumping left and right for 12 reps total.

Tips and Progressions

- When first trying the exercise, start by jumping small distances while your partner delays the push, letting you land and stabilize your posture before pushing on the ball.
- Progress by jumping greater distances, increasing the lateral loading.
- Next, your partner applies pushes as soon as you touch the floor from your lateral jump. To land safely, secure a positive angle, planting the outside foot out past the hips. Dorsiflex, pulling the toe up, to create a heel lock before hitting the floor, which helps prevent inversion sprains.
- To impose varied overload on the body, you can also use a DSL stability ball. When you land the lateral jump, the load inside the ball will shift so that your core also has to brace for the impact while the shoulders carry the weighted ball against gravity.

a

b

This exercise activates all of the upper-body and core muscle groups for stabilization throughout the exercise. It is a great way to overload the muscles without loading up Olympic weights.

Setup

Standing behind the ball, place your hands on the ball at shoulder width. Shuffle your feet back until your chest is over the ball and you are supported on your toes.

Movement

Bend at the elbows to lower your chest to the ball, slowly lowering to 90 degrees at the elbows. Maintain a strongly contracted core; do not let your hips relax and sag. Hold for two seconds at the bottom. Keep your shoulders and hips square.

Finish

Extend your arms to bring your upper body back to the setup position.

Tips and Progressions

- In the push-up position, lift one foot off the floor and work to balance as you lower and push up.
- At the setup stage, place your hands on the side of the ball. Press into the ball as you lower and raise your body.

a

b

REVERSE BALANCE PUSH-UP

 An elevated foot placement moves more of the load to your upper body and requires more core and hip stability. We recommend this exercise in combination with balance push-ups.

Setup

Standing behind the ball, crouch down and place your abdominals on top of the ball. Roll forward until your hands reach the floor in front of the ball. Walk your hands out until only your feet remain on top of the ball. Contract the core to hold a strong link—your body should be in a straight and firm line from feet to head.

Movement

As you bend at the elbows to lower your chest to the floor, maintain your balance on the ball. Keep your torso facing square to the floor.

Finish

Hold for one second at the bottom, and then extend your arms to bring your upper body back to the setup position.

Tips and Progressions

Once in the setup position, have a spotter position a balance board under your hands to produce dual instability. As you lower into the push-up, you must keep your feet balanced on the ball while also balancing your arms on the board. Your core must be strongly contracted to link the body together from its positions of instability.

a

b

This is an excellent exercise for upper-body stability, posterior deltoid strength, arm strength, and trunk and pelvic stability.

Setup

Begin by getting into a prone plank position on the ball with your elbows shoulder-width apart and bent at 90 degrees. Your forearms should be directly on top of the ball. Your feet should be a little wider than shoulder-width apart, and your core is engaged so that your ankles, knees, hips, and shoulders are all in alignment. Engage your core and shoulder stabilizers.

Movement

Lead with the right arm by picking up your right arm and placing your right hand on the ball. Now push up and extend your elbow so that it is fully extended. Immediately after, lift your left elbow off and quickly place your left hand where your left elbow was. While doing this movement, try to keep your hips from rotating side to side.

Middle Position

In the middle position you should be in a prone plank position with your hands on the ball. Your core musculature is engaged to prevent the low back from sagging.

Finish

Engage your core again, and reverse the movement that got you up there. Pick up your right arm, and then place your right elbow where your hand was by using your left arm to lower yourself with control. Lift your left hand off and place your left elbow where your left hand was. Repeat for desired amount of reps. Be sure to do the same in leading the movement with your left arm.

Tips and Progressions

- It sometimes takes a couple of tries to get the feel and rhythm necessary to do the exercise correctly. For this exercise you may want to have a spotter or place the ball against a dumbbell for more stability.
- For a progression, narrow your base of support by bringing your feet closer together.
- Greater challenge comes with slowing the movement overall, with longer loading phases before adding the next movement.
- For those who cannot stabilize the one-arm transitions, a DSL stability ball will provide a more stable base from which to attempt the exercise.

a

b

Every exercise of every kind can be assessed in terms of a ratio of risk to benefit. For example, we do not allow our clients to stand on the ball. Although a few are capable, the risk of a substantial fall and injury is high. Part of the assessment is the exit strategy if things don't go right. There are half-balls called BOSU Balance Trainers with hundreds of standing exercises and a simple step-off exit strategy. With stability balls, we go as far as kneeling on them. Your center of mass remains close to the ball, and to exit, the feet easily slide off the ball and onto the floor. Kneeling holds and clock movements are great for grading force production in different directions and refining control of the hips and abdominals.

Setup

To get up on the ball, place your hands and then knees on the front top part of the ball. Roll forward as you release the hands. Use a narrow leg position and elevate through the rib cage for a tall postural position. Arms can be flexed at your sides, neutral.

On your first attempts at this exercise, have a spotter stand in front of you, one arm flexed. Hold the spotter's forearm to help you get up on the ball and stabilize. Gradually soften your grip on the spotter's arm. The front spotter position is easiest for you to hold and prevents you from coming off the ball forward. The other three exit options—back, to the left, and to the right—are easier for getting a foot down on the floor. Use a wider leg placement to allow adductors to squeeze into the ball to assist in balancing, and keep your hips close to your ankles, lowering your center of mass.

Movement

In your first few sets with this exercise, strive to stay on top of the ball, reacting with any corrective responses needed to deviations in balance. It will mirror a golf swing—just when you think you have it, it becomes difficult again. Use strong bracing and minor adjustments to return the ball to the setup position, weight centered on top.

Tips and Progressions

- If you find it difficult to stay on top of the ball, select a DSL stability ball, which will decrease the instability and help you succeed at the kneeling hold.

- At the other end of the continuum, to advance the drill, purposefully shift your center of mass on the ball, which forces you to contract the correct muscles to the correct degree to return to a centered position. Start with one-inch shifts, shifting to a 3 o'clock position, then 6 o'clock, 9 o'clock, and 12 o'clock. Learn to grade the amount of force you generate so you do not overadjust. On the sideways movements to 3 o'clock and 9 o'clock, gradually increase the amount of displacement until you are striving to find and hold a finish position with one leg on top of the ball, the other leg rolled off to the side as in photo *b*, still alternating from side to side without placing a foot on the floor. This places additional demands on hip strength and control, which are essential for single-leg movements.

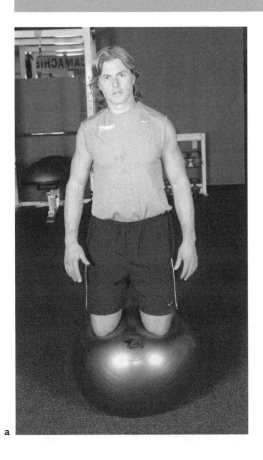 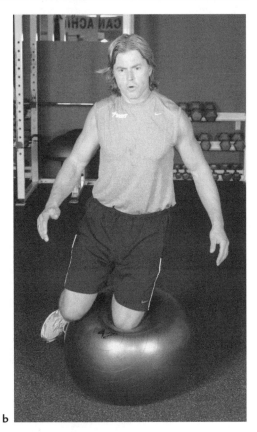

a   b

This is a fun exercise that forces participants to think their way through with keen body awareness.

Setup

Begin kneeling up on the ball—glutes up off the heels, torso up tall, back in a neutral position with the core muscles engaged.

Movement

Start by passing the medicine ball back and forth from one hand to the other with arms out in front of you. Progress by taking the passes up overhead.

Tips and Progressions

- Start off with small short passes and progress to wider passes.
- Progress further by tunneling vision to just the ball as it travels from side to side in front of the body and also up overhead and across to the other side.

SEATED HUMPTY DUMPTY

Have fun with this one! This is a great warm-up exercise that stimulates core strength and responsiveness.

Setup

Begin by sitting up straight on a stability ball with the core muscles engaged. Find a balance point where you can lift your feet a few inches off the floor. To prevent overuse of the hip flexors while in this position, slightly lean back so the angle at the hips is 90 degrees or greater.

Movement

Between two or more people sitting on stability balls, pass a weighted ball back and forth. Do not let the feet touch the floor.

Tips and Progressions

- This is a great icebreaker exercise and can easily be turned into a game. Have fun with this—count the number of successful passes, count how long you can go before someone's foot touches down or how many passes you can get in a time frame, or add a few more medicine balls into the mix.
- You can further progress the exercise by using heavier balls, increasing the distance between the throws, or passing farther from the midline (but still in reach).

KNEELING MEDICINE BALL CATCH

This exercise requires that a dynamic load be caught in an unstable position. By removing the eccentric action of the legs, the entire responsibility to stabilize is left to the core.

Setup

To get up on the ball, place your hands and then the knees on the front top part of the ball. Roll forward as you release the hands. Use a narrow leg position and elevate through the rib cage for a tall postural position. Draw in and brace the core and set the middle back. Extend the arms out at chest level. Your coach or partner positions about 6 feet (1.8 meters) away, directly in front of you.

Movement

Stay as solid as possible on top of the ball, making continuous minor adjustments to any deviations in balance. The coach begins passing the ball directly down the midline, straight to your hands. Flex at the elbows to cushion the catch while you contract through the core, glutes, and adductors to keep your weight centered on the ball. When you have secured a stable position, pass the ball back to the coach, prepare to break momentum after ball release, and stay on top of the ball.

Tips and Progressions

- If this exercise is not manageable, replace it with two exercises: kneeling hold and clock along with medicine ball shoulder-to-shoulder pass (pages 52 and 202). After perfecting the advanced progressions in both of those exercises, try the kneeling medicine ball catch again.

- To work on progressive overload, the coach can deliver passes outside the midline, so you catch in front of one shoulder, making stabilization on top of the ball more difficult.

- Next, the coach positions off to one side to distribute cross-body passes that you catch with two hands in front of the body, allowing slight rotation while maintaining control.

a

b

PROGRESSIVE TABLETOP

This exercise uses a four-point stance to activate the core, integrating instability and reduced base of support to heighten the activation of muscles.

Setup

In a standing position, place your knees in contact with the ball; position your hands on top of the ball. Load your weight onto the hands as you shift your weight forward, bringing the feet off the floor. When in place with a four-point stance, knees are on top of the ball and hands are slightly forward. Draw in and brace your core.

Movement

Contract your glutes, hips, abdominals, back, and shoulders to anchor this position, making minor adjustments to correct any deviations in balance. Focus on retaining a set middle-back position, holding and correcting movement without hunching your shoulders. Lift one arm, holding it straight out parallel to the trunk. Alternate arms.

Tips and Progressions

- Enhance core strength by trying the same maneuver with one leg. Lift a knee and extend the leg behind you, level with hips and parallel to the floor. Glutes will fire aggressively and likewise the shoulders and lats will work hard to hold the position on the ball.

- Once you can hold an extended leg with solid coordination for 20 seconds, you are ready to progress to opposite arm and leg, lifting one arm up and also lifting the opposite leg as shown in photo *b*.

- If you weren't able to achieve the original tabletop on the ball, adopt the progressions listed previously (lift arm, progress to leg, progress to opposite arm or leg), but do them on a mat on the floor. This will help you build the required strength to eventually get back up on the ball into a tabletop position.

a

b

This is an excellent exercise to overload the core through a full range of motion with a natural rolling motion. Rollouts produce eccentric elongation as well as isometric contraction. This exercise also works the chest, back, shoulders, and triceps muscle groups.

Setup

Kneel in front of a ball and produce a pelvic tilt, moving your glutes forward and drawing in your navel toward your spine. Place your hands on top of the ball and bring your feet off of the floor. This allows your knees to become the pivot point. Walk your hands out on the ball, moving the ball and your arms away from your body. Once you feel your abdominals beginning to work you have reached your starting position.

Movement

Now your hands will remain stationary on the ball. Pivot on your knees and bring your torso and hips forward as the ball rolls away from your knees. Keep moving until your chest drops down. Keep your chest upright as much as possible, avoiding the superman pose. If you feel any strain in your lower back, make sure you are not in the superman pose. If your back discomfort remains, return to the setup stage and check your pelvic tilt.

Finish

Hold at the far reach for two seconds then roll back in to the starting position.

Tips and Progressions

- In the extended rollout position, rather than holding stationary for two seconds, move the ball outside of your midline to place additional demands on the core muscles. Try a figure-eight pattern or a side-to-side movement aiming to move your right hand in front of your left shoulder (and left hand to right shoulder on the reverse), or select a word to spell. For example, in the far extended position, move the ball to spell each letter in *power;* that completes one rep before you return to the setup position.

- Progress to a single-arm rollout. Keep the ball positioned down your midline, and remove one hand to perform one-arm kneeling rollouts.

- Complete single-arm kneeling rollouts with the ball positioned outside of midline, more in line with your active arm. This produces additional loading on the shoulder, triceps, and abdominals. Stabilizing muscles have to work harder to prevent hip and torso rotation.

a

b

STANDING ROLLOUT

This is an excellent exercise for challenging core strength. It provides advanced loading and also teaches body awareness and weight-transferring skills. The longer the lever the exerciser produces, the more strength required through the arms.

Setup

Stand in a deep athletic stance with your ankles, knees, and hips flexed in a deep squat and the ball in front of you. Hinge at the hip so that your back is still flat, and place your fingertips on the downslope of the ball (side closest to you). In this position, your weight is loaded on the legs. Your shoulders are over the hands, and glutes are lower than the shoulders.

Movement

Transfer your weight over the hands on the ball, engage your core, and roll the ball forward. As you roll forward, keep your weight loaded onto the hands while you slowly extend from the hips and knees so that your shoulders, hips, and knees are in a more horizontal alignment.

Middle Position

In the middle position you should be in a prone plank position with your back flat, hands on the ball, and legs almost completely extended. Your core musculature is engaged to prevent the low back from sagging.

Finish

Reverse the movement by transferring your weight off of your hands and toes so that the weight is evenly distributed on your feet and your fingertips are back to the downslope of the ball.

Tips and Progressions

For this exercise you might want to start with slow movements to maintain posture as well as have more time under tension for the anterior compartment of the core. Start off with very small rollouts, then progress to longer rollouts, working toward full extension of the knees, hips, and shoulders.

a

b

This exercise provides a fun and interesting challenge. Less attention is focused on body technique; rather, participants will discover the right mechanics as they explore how to stay on the balls. This generates very thorough activation of the musculature through the shoulders, back, abdominals, and hips, all of which must work extremely hard to complete each rep. You will need to handle the load of your body weight and prevent sideways movement of the ball, with reactive muscle contractions to correct losses of balance.

Setup

Select two different sized balls, and set them about 6 inches (15 centimeters) apart. Set the heels of your hands on the top outside of the front 65-centimeter ball, while you mount the knees on the back 55-centimeter ball. Establish a kneeling position, hips low, hands on the front ball, and set the mid back.

Movement

Shift some of your weight onto the hands, and work to hold this position without exiting the balls. React to any deviations in balance by pulling back to a centered position.

Tips and Progressions

- After you learn how to stay up on the two balls with fewer movement deviations, progress to a dual-ball rollout where you extend the arms and legs to create more separation between the balls. Start by moving both balls 1 inch (2.5 centimeters) and return to the set up position.

- Progress over a number of workouts to longer extension, moving the balls as far apart as possible, as shown in the photo.

- If you reach a distance that is uncomfortable on the lumbar spine, shorten the distance you will work, potentially reverting to the static survival hold position. Also add supplemental supine bridge and prone extension exercises to prepare the back to handle greater challenges.

FULL-BODY MULTIJOINT MEDICINE BALL PASS

 This exercise produces sequential full-body power as well as anaerobic conditioning.

Setup

Stand facing your partner, about six paces apart. Keep your feet shoulder-width apart, knees slightly flexed, and abdominals precontracted.

Movement

Before you pass the ball, squat down and touch the ball to the floor. The pass begins from this position. Maintain a good squat position, chest up and back in a safe position. The throw begins with the legs and transfers through the hips and on to the upper body. The force–ground relationship is important here, because you will need to finish with a powerful leg extension, jumping right off the floor.

Remember the desired ball direction is forward, not just up, so you must drive up and out (forward) to direct the force in the intended direction.

Finish

Your partner should not attempt to catch this long-distance pass. Through trial and error, your partner will be positioned to allow the ball to land on the floor and catch it on the bounce, which is safer and easier on the body. After receiving the ball, your partner squats and touches the ball to the floor before driving up and forward with the entire body to pass a maximal distance. Every pass is a "best effort." You try to work your partner backward, throwing a longer distance with all of your power.

Tips and Progressions

- Get twisted lateral two-ball pass: This drill uses the same throw technique. Both partners start with a medicine ball at opposite sides of the drill course. On "Go," both throw for maximal distance. Then immediately begin a quick lateral shuffle to the other side, where you will pick up your partner's ball and throw it back, right from the floor with a full-body squat throw.

- Continue throwing for maximal distance and shuffling at maximal speed for 30 seconds. As your anaerobic conditioning improves, increase the drill time. The intensity of this drill is 110 percent.

a

b

MEDICINE BALL BALANCE CATCH

This exercise focuses on proprioception and balance during the eccentric loading and catch phase as well as the isometric postcatch position. It is a great way to integrate the entire body together without having to handle an advanced load or advanced speed of movement.

Setup

Both partners stand on a balance board, facing each other, about two paces apart. Keep your feet shoulder-width apart with knees slightly flexed and abdominals pre-contracted.

Movement

Send each other light passes aimed at chest level and within the boundaries of each shoulder.

Finish

Receive the pass with a strong core and legs, attempting to catch the ball, retain your balance, and remain square to your partner. Be sure the knees stay in line over the ankles (not dropping in). Hold this balanced position for two seconds before returning the pass.

Tips and Progressions

- Full-body catch with static hold: Complete the same exercise setup. Upon catching the ball, progress into a full squat on the balance board. Hold the squat at the bottom for three seconds before rising up under control and returning the pass to your partner.

- Catches outside center of gravity: Complete the same exercise setup. Aim your light passes outside of your partner's center of gravity. Deliver passes outside of the shoulder boundary (off to the side). Send low passes, overhead passes, and short passes that fall in front of your partner. The catch-and-balance response is more challenging and fun.

- Catch the ball and move back to a strong posture position with good balance before returning the pass.

From a bridge position, a second ball is used for a variety of dynamic stabilizing load movements to foster reactive muscle capabilities through the eccentric-concentric responses.

Setup

Assume a supine bridge position on top of a ball. Feet are in a narrow stance, hips up strong, core set. Hold a DSL stability ball up over the chest, arms extended.

Movement

1. Keeping the arms close to full extension, complete small and large circles with fluid, consistent movement so you can hear the DSL flow around the ball.

2. Shift the DSL stability ball side to side, moving wider and faster until you accommodate with torso rotation. Listen for the impact of the DSL traveling across the ball, which you will also feel as you brace for the impact of the DSL.

3. Complete a sit-up pattern. Sit up and extend the arms in front of your chest. Sit back down into the supine bridge position, arms out over head. Again, absorb the force of the DSL as it shifts across to the other side of the ball at each end range of motion.

Tips and Progressions

- Begin with smaller ranges of motion and regress by keeping the ball closer to your torso.
- Progress by adding more load to the ball.

a

b

SUPINE BRIDGE BALL HOLD

The supine bridge is one of the foundational ball positions that so many exercises build from, effectively developing the deep core musculature plus obliques, shoulders, pecs, low back, glutes, and hamstrings.

Setup

Begin in bridge position with feet flat on the floor and spaced hip-width apart. Knees are at 90 degrees, and head and shoulders are fully supported on the stability ball. Arms are extended, holding a medicine ball directly above the chest. Elbows are bent slightly but locked in position. Keep the hips up and core engaged.

Movement

Your partner stands behind your head to apply three-second pushes on the medicine ball, alternating left and right. Your goal is to keep the core locked in and not allow any movement in the arms or core. On the second set, shift to rapid-fire pushes, delivering a strong, quick push immediately followed by a push in the opposite direction, continuing for 20 seconds.

Tips and Progressions

- If the medicine ball deviates far outside the midline, ease up on the push.
- Most partners err by pushing too lightly. Push with enough force so that your partner has to struggle to maintain the medicine ball position.
- Athletes who are extremely strong in the bridge position can also be challenged by
  1. bringing the feet closer together to lessen the base of support,
  2. closing the eyes, or
  3. varying the direction of the medicine ball push (left, right, forward, back, diagonal).

In this integrated exercise, you work a squat pattern and transition to supine, where you complete a sit-up.

Setup

Begin with your DSL stability ball in neutral position (label up). The DSL stability ball has circle markings that you can use as a reference point to complete the supine portion without ball movement and to define a spot to aim for that will help you avoid falling off the ball.

Standing with your back toward the DSL stability ball, squat down so that your glutes touch at about the outer edge of the large top circle. Sit down on the top front side of the DSL stability ball, and position the feet so that the upper legs are parallel to the floor with the feet in a shoulder-width stance. You might have to adjust the distance you are standing from the ball to find the correct position.

Movement

Without any arm swing, come up to a standing position, then squat back down until the glutes rest back on the top front side of the ball. Lower the torso under control into a supine bridge position. Lift one leg off the floor and hold for three seconds; repeat with other leg.

Finish

With both feet on the floor, slowly lift your torso off the ball, segment by segment, rising up to a seated position before standing.

Tips and Progressions

- The ball does not roll during this exercise. It should remain in a neutral position, which you can check by starting the exercise with the logo at the top.
- Repeat the sequence for a desired rep count; however, as you close in on the finishing reps, fatigue may determine that you eliminate the leg lift portion so you can effectively continue with the squat to sit-up and finish strong.

a

b

c

Left-to-right exercise produces excellent balance and proprioception responses while overloading the speed center. The deep abdominal wall and core abdominal muscles contribute through eccentric loading, stabilization, and concentric action. The single-leg stance accelerates the demands on the speed center. You will feel every muscle working from toes to abdominals.

Setup

Stand on one leg with knee slightly flexed. Set the abdominals and focus on balance. Hold the ball with two hands in front of your body.

Movement

Move the ball over to the left side of your body, but do not rotate the torso. The torso and shoulders should remain square, facing straight forward. Move the ball back across the body and over to the right side of the body.

Finish

Continue to move the ball alternately from the left to right sides of your body, reacting to the changing load position by contracting the abs, hips, and legs. Your degree of knee flexion will adjust appropriately to counterbalance the shifting load positioning.

Tips and Progressions

- Increase the speed of movement.
- Move the ball farther away from the body, farther off to the side, and farther in front of the body upon rotation.
- Toss the ball from the left hand to the right hand as shown in the photo. Catch and absorb with the arm, core, and leg. This increases the balance challenge and also increases the load on the abdominals. This is an excellent abdominal exercise.
- Rapid-fire toss: Move the ball from the left hand to the right hand as quickly as possible.

SINGLE-LEG MEDICINE BALL SELF-PASS AND TRACKING

This exercise develops independent leg strength and balance, linking the deceleration core strength in a standing position, and eye–hand coordination. The weight of the ball and the visual tracking add to the balance challenge.

Setup

Begin standing on one leg with the knee slightly bent, the quads and glutes engaged, and core and middle back set.

Movement

Start by passing the medicine ball back and forth from one hand to the other with arms out in front of you. Maintain a steady setup posture, avoid rotating the torso during each catch, and keep the eyes forward. After catching 10 passes back and forth between your left and right hand, vary the height of the catches, increase the distance, and begin to visually track the ball. As you track the ball passes from the left and right side, make sure the eyes follow.

Tips and Progressions

- Start off with small, short passes and progress to wider passes.
- Then try taking the passes up overhead.

STEP AND PUSH BACK

This power exercise loads the core and trains sequential firing between the legs, hips, abdominals, and upper extremities.

Setup

Stand with feet at shoulder width, facing your partner. Assume an athletic-ready position. Your partner holds a small medicine ball.

Movement

Your partner delivers a pass directly to one shoulder. As the ball approaches, step forward with one leg.

Finish

Upon making contact with the ball, immediately *push* the ball away from the body, straight out from your shoulder and back to your partner. Return to a ready position. Continue for a set number of reps.

Tips and Progressions

Upon making ball contact and initiating the push, remember your hips and core—the speed center—must get behind this action and assist in the force production.

a

b

ONE-LEG OPPOSITE-ARM MEDICINE BALL PASS

This exercise teaches you to decelerate and catch with the entire body while building posterior deltoid, pectoral, core, hip, and leg strength to catch and balance on one leg. Ultimately, body position relies heavily on core stability during all positions of the exercise.

Setup

Begin facing a partner at least 6 feet (1.8 meters) apart. Each partner stands on the same single leg (for example, both stand on the left leg). Partner A holds a medicine ball at the shoulder opposite the standing support leg. Partner B presents a target with arm extended and hand open, preparing to receive the ball. Partner B will tend to set up with the hand close to the shoulder; make sure he or she has the hand out away from the body ready to receive the ball. To initiate movement, partner A preloads the leg by dropping body mass two inches (five centimeters) before extending the leg, transferring power from the leg through the core and out through the arm.

Movement

Partner A passes the medicine ball across to partner B. Partner B receives the pass, catching by flexing the arm, braking with the core, and flexing at the knee and ankle to absorb the weight of the ball. Keep the chest up, shoulders back, and core engaged to avoid excess rotation. Before returning the pass, take time to regain balance and ensure the knee tracks in line with the toes and over the ankle. Alternate the standing leg on passes.

Tips and Progressions

- Use a slow movement tempo, counting two seconds on the concentric and eccentric phases. Pause in the middle to perfect a single-leg balanced position.
- Slow catching mechanics will prove more difficult from a strength, stability, and balance perspective.
- For even greater adaptations, slow down the catch sequence and shift into a deeper leg position.
- To increase the transferability to sport skills, decrease the coupling time between the catch and pass (eccentric–concentric phases) and increase the tempo and the power of the throw.

Core
Rotation

Exercises in This Chapter

RUSSIAN TWIST

The Russian twist is an excellent exercise for integrating static extension and rotational trunk movement. Movement of this nature occurs in many situations, including football, rugby, hockey, and tennis.

Setup

Sitting on a ball, walk forward, allowing the ball to roll underneath you. Keep walking out until your head and shoulders are supported by the ball. Arms should be extended over your chest, your abdominals set, and your core parallel to the floor.

Movement

Begin by rotating all the way to one side. Ensure rotation is initiated by the core. Many first-timers to the Russian twist will initiate rotation from the shoulder. It is also important to keep your eyes on your hands, enhancing the total core rotation as you move.

Finish

As you reach your end range, change direction and then begin moving in the opposite direction.

Tips and Progressions

- Hold a medicine ball or dumbbell in hand.
- By setting up in front of an adjustable cable, you will obtain greater loading in both directions as a result of the constant loading from the cable.

a

b

The diagonal firing patterns associated with the catch–throw phase link the shoulder and opposite hip with a core pattern that is transferable to many activities.

Setup

Partner A is in a supine bridge position: shoulders on the ball, neck supported and neutral, hips up, and feet hip-width apart and firmly planted on the floor. Feet should be positioned far enough out so the knee joint is at 90 degrees and not shooting out over the toes. With a medicine ball in the hands, arms are extended up in line with the chest. Partner B stands to the right of partner A about 5 feet (1.5 meters) away in a good athletic stance, ready to give and receive the medicine ball passes.

Start Position

Partner A rotates from the core onto the left shoulder, keeping the hips squared and feet planted, dropping the hands (with medicine ball) off to the left side in line with the shoulders.

Movement

Partner A rotates from the left shoulder around to the right, releasing the ball to partner B. Partner A decelerates the rotational movement to the right so that partner A can receive the pass back from partner B and return to the start position. Repeat the exercise going from the right to the left.

BACK-TO-BACK STOP-AND-GO

 This is a great torso rotation exercise that also works the muscles eccentrically, building braking strength. Stopping and reversing direction help to overload the torso musculature.

Setup

With a partner, stand back to back, about 6 inches (15 centimeters) apart. Keep your feet shoulder-width apart, knees slightly flexed, and abdominals precontracted.

Movement

It is important to clearly differentiate this exercise from the Back-to-Back 180-Degree Rotation Pass. In the Stop-and-Go execution, once you pass the ball, you stay in place awaiting the ball to be returned. This helps focus the effort on a strong rotation rep and an aggressive eccentric–concentric coupling when the direction is reversed. Holding the ball out away from the body, partner A rotates around to the right with speed and abruptly stops the ball off to the side, quickly returning to the left to pass the ball off to the partner. Partner B picks up the ball on the right side and immediately rotates with speed to the left. Once all the way around to the left side, partner B stops abruptly and quickly rotates back to the original (right) side to drop off the ball.

Finish

Continue this sequence for a set number of repetitions. Repeat the opposite way around.

Tips and Progressions

- Move your feet right together, and keep your knees bent.
- Move the ball farther away from your body.
- Rotate with greater speed.
- Stop more quickly.

This exercise builds full-body power and torso rotation and produces sequential muscle firing for a smooth multijoint throw. Multijoint power in a closed kinetic chain through a transverse plane applies to many sports and activities.

Setup

Stand facing away from a partner, about two paces apart. Keep your feet shoulder-width apart, knees well flexed, and abdominals precontracted. Your partner is facing you (looking at your back), one step to the right.

Movement

Before you throw the ball, squat down and rotate to bring the ball in front of your right shin. The throw initiates from this position. Be sure to use a squat movement, dropping your hips to lower the ball to shin height so there is not excessive forward trunk flexion. The throw begins at the foot, transfers through your right leg, and transfers through the hips and torso and on to the upper body.

Remember the desired ball direction is behind to your partner, not just up, so you must rotate through the torso and follow through behind you to direct the ball from above your left shoulder to your partner, who is standing behind you and off to your right.

Finish

Your partner catches the ball and rolls it back to your right side, where you can pick it up and move into the sequential throw technique. Repeat for the desired number of repetitions, then repeat the exercise throwing over the opposite (right) shoulder. Your partner will change his position, staying two paces behind you but shifting to your left side.

Tips and Progressions

After you release the throw, keep your hands up above your shoulders. Your partner will catch your throw and return a gentle pass into your hands, where you catch it above your shoulders, rotate, and squat to the opposite side. Then thrust upward to throw the ball back over the same shoulder.

a

b

This exercise places a weight at the end of a lever arm to increase the demands of the torso to stabilize and direct movement.

Setup

Lie on the floor in a supine position with your arms straight out to the sides. Make sure you achieve a solid pelvic tilt. Set the abdominals before lifting the legs into the air. Legs are together and flexed to 90 degrees. Place a small medicine ball between your knees. Press inward to hold the ball in place and activate your adductors and hip musculature.

Movement

Slowly lower the knees under control, off to the right side. Shoulders and back must remain flat on the floor.

Finish

Lift the legs back up over your hips (still flexed) and onward to the left side. Lower to the left. Stop and return. Continue for desired number of reps or until you lose neutral torso supine position.

Tips and Progressions

- Complete the same sequence with more speed. Drop legs to the left, and activate muscles to decelerate and stop before touching the floor. Return across the body to the opposite side.

- Position the legs into a straight position over the body and position the ball between the ankles to increase the lever arm and place the loading farther out on the lever.

a

b

93

Supine scissors will place a great challenge on the abdominals from a static perspective.

Setup

Lying on the floor, place a ball between your feet and ankles; squeeze. Place your hands under your back at the L3 (mid-lumbar) level of your spine, engage your core, and maintain the pressure you feel on your hands.

Movement

Begin by raising your feet and the ball so to create a 45-degree angle at your hips. While squeezing the ball, rotate at your hips so that one foot rotates over the other.

Finish

Return to the start position and rotate to the opposite side.

Tips and Progressions

- If you do not have the shoulder flexibility to place your hands under your low back, leave them by your sides, and consciously think about pressing your spine into the floor.
- You can progress this movement by raising and lowering the legs and ball after each rotation.

a

b

PRONE TWIST

The prone twist will combine a challenge in both the sagittal and transverse planes. This movement will tie in the hips, shoulders, and core.

Setup

Begin with the ball under your abdomen and hands on the floor in a push-up position. Walk your hands forward so the ball begins to roll toward your feet. At this point, widen your feet over the ball, and squeeze. Your shoulders and core must be firing before you initiate the movement.

Movement

Laterally roll the ball to one side by rotating your hips.

Finish

Hold end range for a second, then return and rotate to the opposite side.

Tips and Progressions

Most errors in the prone twist occur as you begin the movement. What you need to avoid is a drop in the low back. By keeping your core engaged, you will feel the work of the lower portion of your abdominals. The low back should be held in a neutral position or should be slightly kyphotic (rounded).

a

b

GOLDY'S STATIC LATERAL HELICOPTER

 The static lateral helicopter was developed as a progression from the abdominal side crunch.

Setup

Set up this movement with your feet at the base of the wall and floor. Your bottom leg should be forward and top leg braced back as you sit laterally on the ball. Placement on the ball should be so that your hips are at the apex of the ball. Core should be in a position so that there is a straight line from the ear to the shoulders, hips, and knees.

Movement

While you're holding the static lean position, your arms should be extended and level with your shoulders. Begin the movement by rotating your upper core as far as you can turn. Maintain your arm position as you rotate so your arms resemble a helicopter blade. Do not turn your head as you rotate. Keep your eyes focused straight up to the ceiling.

Finish

Complete your repetitions to one side, then repeat on the other.

Tips and Progressions

You can increase the difficulty of this movement by holding dumbbells in each hand. You will find that two to five pounds (about one to just over two kilograms) will be quite challenging.

a

b

This is a good warm-up exercise that gently works the legs, hips, torso, and upper body. With more powerful passes, it is a great torso rotation strength exercise, pertinent to so many sports.

Setup

Partners are four strides apart, both facing the same wall. One partner has a medicine ball. Feet are positioned shoulder-width apart, knees flexed, abdominals set, head turned to see partner.

Movement

All parts of the body work together to produce the rotation pass. Push off your outside foot, and transfer the force through the hips and into torso rotation while the arms draw the ball across your body. Release the ball with a full follow-through, aiming the ball so your partner can catch it in front of the body.

Finish

Catch the ball with a strong core to protect the lower back. Absorb the catch by flexing the knee of the outside leg, rotating the torso to the outside, and allowing the arms to travel across the body to an exaggerated position off to the side. Stop and reverse the process to return the pass to your partner.

Tips and Progressions

Static catch: Flex the knees a little more to prepare to catch the ball in front of your body, and use the abdominals to completely brake the path of the ball. Catch the ball and stop its travel right in front of your body. Once stationary, move back into the normal catch reception movement to prepare to throw the ball back to your partner.

a

b

V-SIT AND ROTATE

This is simply a good abdominal exercise that prepares the torso for more dynamic rotation exercises and more intense eccentric loading.

Setup

Sit on the floor, leaning back one-third of the way into a sit-up. Feet remain on the floor, knees flexed. Hold a medicine ball in front of your body.

Movement

Rotate off to the left and touch the ball to the floor. Rotate around as far as comfortably possible and touch the floor out and away from your body.

Finish

Lift the ball back off the floor, and rotate around to the right, carrying the ball across the body and touching it to the floor off to the right.

Tips and Progressions

- The farther away from the body the ball is carried, and the farther away from the body the ball is touched to the floor, the greater the load on the abdominals.
- An intense progression involves lifting the feet off the floor. Maintain knee flexion to 90 degrees, hold the legs together and feet together, and complete the same exercise holding the feet a few inches in the air. You will need a stronger core to lift the ball back off the floor and a stronger core to stabilize the body and hold a V-sit position while rotating.

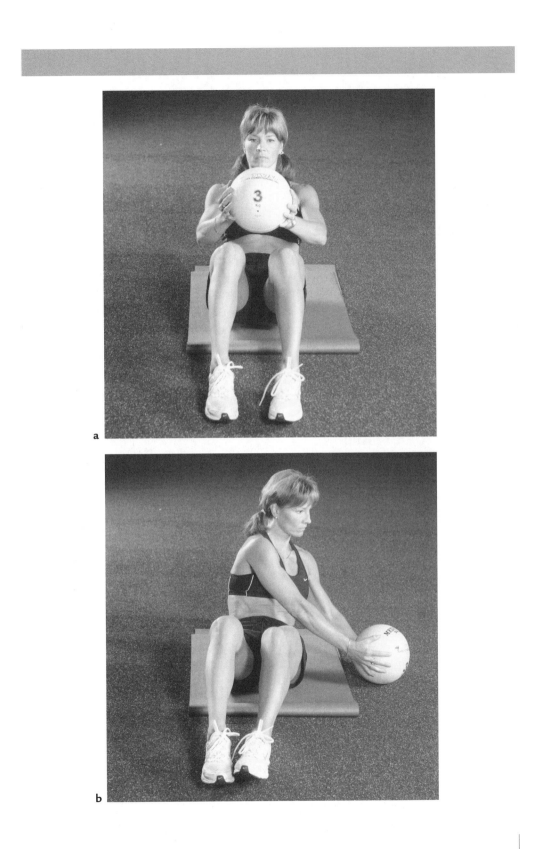

a

b

BACK-TO-BACK 180-DEGREE ROTATION PASS

Standing torso rotation is a vital movement pattern to overload and strengthen in preparation for sport actions and daily activity.

Setup

With a partner, stand back to back, about 6 inches (15 centimeters) apart. Keep your feet shoulder-width apart, knees slightly flexed, and abdominals precontracted.

Movement

Partner A rotates to the right and drops off the ball at the side to partner B, who is picking it up on the left side. Partner B receives the ball and holds it far away from the torso, out away from the body. Partner B rotates to the right and passes the ball to partner A, who receives it to the left. A key to this exercise is maintaining a strong core and bent knees so that the rotation comes from the hips and abdominals. You should feel your core "leading" the way.

Finish

Continue this sequence for a set number of repetitions. Then repeat the opposite way around.

Tips and Progressions

360-degree rotation passes: Partners move about 2 feet (61 centimeters) apart and remain back to back. The extra distance allows room for the ball and hip movement, because the pass will transfer behind the back between partners. Partner A rotates to the right and continues twisting to position the ball behind the back. Partner B rotates to the opposite side, rotating to the right to pick up the pass behind the back. Partner B next rotates to the left, holding the ball out away from the body. After dropping off the ball, partner A rotates to the left to be in position to receive the ball back.

a   b

This exercise links the core to the shoulders and rotator cuff group for a functional pattern used in daily activity and sport.

Setup

Begin in a standing position with feet shoulder-width apart. Core is set and braced, middle back is set. Hold a DSL stability ball at mid-torso height, hands pressing inward.

Movement

Squat with a lateral weight shift, lowering the ball to the same side to knee height. Counteract that movement by rotating in the opposite direction. Bring the ball out and around the torso.

Finish

Release the outside heel to achieve triple leg extension and to encourage full hip action. Finish with the ball up over the shoulder on the opposite side.

Tips and Progressions

- Begin with a slow, smooth action back and forth so that you hear a steady flow of DSL *around* the ball.
- After several workouts, begin to increase the velocity of movement from low to high, shifting the DSL *across* the ball. This will encourage additional bracing and shoulder stabilization to prepare for the impact of the DSL as it hits the other side of the ball.

a

b

Closed kinetic chain rotary power and eccentric braking are trained through perturbations provided by the dynamic stabilizing load inside the ball. This builds strength and helps prevent sport injury.

Setup

Begin in a standing position, feet shoulder-width apart, and knees flexed. Core is set and braced; middle back is set. Hold a DSL stability ball at mid-torso height, hands pressing inward. Double-check for scapular retraction.

Movement

Rapidly shift the ball side to side for a two-inch (five-centimeter) distance, staying close to the midline. Brake and immediately shift back to the original side. Alternate sides in quick succession. Keep the hips square as the torso rotates slightly.

Tips and Progressions

- Check your speed and force of movement with audible feedback—you should hear the DSL hitting the side of the ball as you brake at the end of each range of motion.

- Progressively increase the rotation distance until eventually you move the ball outside the torso (see photo). As the range increases and greater torso rotation is needed, allow the hips to pivot as well, linking into the core.

- As distance joins speed and force, you will be required to apply stronger deceleration to brake when the DSL strikes against the ball.

MEDICINE BALL STANDING TWIST AGAINST WALL

This movement will assist you with increasing your rotational range of motion around the core.

Setup

Set up in front of a wall by placing your feet shoulder-width apart, approximately 6 to 8 inches (15 to 20 centimeters) from the wall. Your glutes should be in contact with the wall, and you can hold a medicine ball in front at mid-chest level.

Movement

Rotate your core from the start position so that the ball makes contact with the wall.

Finish

Come off the wall explosively, and rotate to the opposite side. Again, come off the wall explosively and repeat.

Tips and Progressions

- To increase the difficulty and progress with your range of motion, you can move your body forward off the wall. By doing this, you will increase the range of motion that is required of your core to turn and get the ball to the wall.

- Once you have progressed your range of motion, you can continue to progress by wrapping the ball in a towel and completing the movement by bouncing the ball hard off the wall.

Legs and Hips

Exercises in This Chapter

HIP EXTENSION AND KNEE FLEXION

 This is the only exercise that can work your hamstrings as both a knee flexor and hip extensor, making this an extremely functional and productive exercise.

Setup

Lying supine on the floor, place a ball under your heels. Arms are in a T position to assist in balance.

Movement

Initiate movement by squeezing your glutes and raising your hips off the floor. Once you reach the position in which your ankles, knees, and hips are in line, bring your heels toward you by flexing your knees.

Finish

Once your heels have gone to their end range, reverse the movement. Extend the knees, then lower your hips.

Tips and Progressions

The following are some progressions that you can work into your program:

- Move your arms in from a T position to your sides.
- Use a larger ball to increase your range of motion and improve balance.
- Add a cable or surgical tubing around your ankle to increase the load as your knees flex.
- Use a single-leg movement instead of a double-leg movement.

a

b

KNEE TUCK

This exercise targets the lower abdominals and hip flexors by having you lift a loaded ball.

Setup

Lie flat on the floor, supine. Back is flat, core is set, and legs are extended. Hold a DSL stability ball between the feet. Rest your arms alongside your torso.

Movement

Keep your back and hips on the floor as you flex the knees to draw the feet toward your body. Tuck the knees in tight over your torso; pause.

Finish

Extend the legs under control, allowing the heels to touch the floor at the extreme range.

Tips and Progressions

- Initially it may be necessary to place your arms out to the sides for stability or to press the arms into the floor during the lift phase. Eventually your goal is to keep your arms relaxed during the lower-body lift.
- If you note excessive lumbar arch or back discomfort, try wedging your hands underneath the glutes.
- If the loaded ball is too heavy, you lose your anchored position, or you still experience low back discomfort, regress to an unweighted ABS ball and complete supplemental ball bridge exercises.

SUPINE LEG CABLE CURL

The supine leg curl is another great method of working the hamstrings from both the hips and the knees.

Setup

Place the ball under your shoulders. Hold on to a cable or surgical tubing placed behind your head. Make sure that your heels are on a nonslip surface or that you can place your heels in front of something solid, such as a weight bar.

Movement

The movement begins by bringing the hips up so that the body is parallel to the floor. Once you are in this position, flex your knees, rolling forward on the ball.

Finish

Once you have rolled as far forward as possible, while maintaining good posture and form, return by extending at the knees. As you come back to full knee extension, do not drop your hips, but prepare to go into the next repetition.

a

b

This is called a "poor man's" exercise because there is no expensive glute ham raise bench involved in performing this exercise. It is an excellent movement that focuses on the hamstrings, glutes, and low back.

Setup

Kneel in front of a ball and perform a pelvic tilt, moving your glutes forward and drawing in your navel toward your spine. Place your hands on top of the ball, and have a partner hold your ankles down. As with the kneeling rollout, instead of your core doing the work, the focus is on your hamstrings and posterior chain.

Movement

Your hands remain stationary on the ball. Pivot on your knees, and bring your torso and hips forward as the ball rolls away from your knees. Contract your hamstrings by applying pressure upward on your partner's hands with your ankles. This results in eccentric lengthening of your hamstrings.

Finish

Once you have loaded yourself eccentrically, contract your hamstrings and pull yourself back up to the starting position. Do not release the pressure you exert into your partner's hands.

The split squat is a great overall exercise for all muscles in the legs and hips. It also requires the postural muscles to fire to keep the torso upright and square.

Setup

Stand in front of a ball and place the laces of your left shoe back on top of the ball. Shuffle your right foot forward and shift your weight onto this support leg. Your front foot points forward so that your knee tracks straight over the ankle. Contract your core to hold a strong balance position.

Movement

Drop your hips and roll your left leg back until the support leg is flexed to 90 degrees. Hold this position for two seconds. Make sure the knee of your support leg is not past your toes. If it is, your stance is too short. To correct, shuffle your support foot farther forward.

Finish

Using the muscles in your support leg, extend the leg to elevate your body back to the setup position. Stay strong and centered to avoid any torso sway as you come back up. Rep out your set, switch legs, and repeat.

Tips and Progressions

- Beginners need a light spot on the ball. The spotter places a hand on each side of the ball to help stabilize the ball.
- For an advanced progression, place the front support foot on a balance board to create dual instability.

a

b

The squat is a foundational strength exercise from which many other leg exercises build. Wall squats are technically easier to execute and allow those with low back problems to participate. This exercise encourages a deeper range of motion and static holds at the bottom while retaining a solid postural position.

Setup

Begin facing away from the wall. Place a stability ball between the wall and your back, positioned level with the lumbar vertebrae. Lean your weight against the ball and adjust your feet, shuffling them out away from your body. Ensure a shoulder-width stance with the feet forward and toes pointed slightly outward.

Movement

To initiate movement, press the heels into the floor to engage the deep abdominal wall. Set the core before slowly lowering your hips toward the floor, flexing the knees until the tibias are perpendicular to the floor with a 90-degree angle at the knees.

Middle Position

In the middle position you should feel a strong load in the quads and glutes while the knees are working but comfortable. Eyes look straight forward, and neck is in a neutral position. If you sense too much strain on the knees, visually check to ensure your knees are not out past your toes. If they are, readjust your setup position by moving the feet farther away from the body.

Finish

Extend the legs to push the body back up the wall to a standing position. Retain pressure against the ball during the entire range of motion.

Tips and Progressions

- Use a slow movement tempo, counting two seconds on the concentric and eccentric phases.
- To advance the challenge, integrate a static hold at the middle position for each repetition, holding that deep stance for three to five seconds before rising back up.
- To emphasize the core, lift one foot two centimeters (less than an inch) off the floor during each static hold, focusing on retaining a level pelvis.
- To increase the strength demands, hold dumbbells at your sides with arms slightly flexed and palms facing in toward the body.

a   b

OVERHEAD LATERAL MEDICINE BALL SQUAT

This exercise works one of the most important physical characteristics for the spine and hips: mobility. People with poor spinal and hip mobility will have a great challenge to complete this correctly. This is an excellent exercise to include as part of your daily warm-up for posture reinforcement.

Setup

Begin by holding a medicine ball overhead with your arms fully extended. There should be no bend in the elbows. Feet are right beside each other to begin the movement.

Movement

Drop your hips and slide one leg out while maintaining the overhead ball position. Do not allow your shoulders to roll forward or your lower back to lose its lordotic curve as you slide to one side.

Finish

Once you have slid to one side, reverse the direction and come back the opposite direction. This is the equivalent of one repetition.

Tips and Progressions

- An effective cue is to imagine there is a string overhead that you must go under while maintaining good posture.
- Another great cue is to use a long piece of dowel rod and have someone hold it over your arms to provide a positional goal to reach.

LATERAL WALL SQUAT

The lateral wall squat builds sport-specific strength, replicating the angles needed for lateral movement and stopping. The glutes, hamstrings, and quadriceps are the main targets of this exercise.

Setup

Stand sideways beside a wall. Position a stability ball against the wall at elbow height. Lean against the ball at a 45-degree angle, your outside leg supporting your body weight.

Movement

Lower into a one-leg squat position, maintaining the 45-degree angle and leaning into the ball. As you flex your knee and lower your hips, the ball will move from elbow height to shoulder height. Keep your hips and shoulders as square as possible.

Finish

Using the muscles in your support leg, extend the leg to elevate your body back to the setup position.

Tips and Progressions

To increase the difficulty of the exercise, repeat the exercise using your inside leg.

O'BRIEN HIP EXTENSION WITH STATIC HIP FLEXION

The O'Brien hip extension was shown to me by Andy O'Brien, a strength coach for the Florida Panthers, during a training camp. It is an excellent exercise that focuses on maintaining pelvic position while working the glutes.

Setup

Begin in a prone position over the ball with both hands placed on the floor to provide a base. The right leg should be flexed with the knee pressing into the ball with approximately 30 percent effort. This static hip flexion will offset the hip extension on the opposite side to maintain a solid pelvis.

Movement

Once your knee is solidly placed into the ball, begin by firing your left glute and extending the left leg.

Middle Position

The left leg should be extended to a point at which the knee, hip, and shoulder create a straight line. Hold this position for two to three seconds.

Finish

After holding the middle position, slowly lower the leg to the start position without releasing the right flexed hip into the ball. Complete your repetitions on the left leg, then reverse the position for the right leg.

Tips and Progressions

If you feel tension or pain in your lower back, this may be a result of weak gluteal muscles. You should check with a therapist or doctor for direction if you have pain.

a

b

PUSH-UP POSITION HIP OPENER

This can truly be called a functional exercise because it challenges the body in the sagittal and transverse planes in a single exercise. You will feel the work throughout your abdominals, shoulders, hip adductors, and extensors. This exercise allows you to work on total-body stability along with hip mobility and rotation.

Setup

Place both hands on top of the stability ball, with feet on the floor in a push-up position. Ensure that your abdominals are engaged and your low back is flat, not lordotic (swayed).

Movement

While holding the push-up position, flex your right hip forward until you reach a 90-degree angle of flexion at the hip and knee.

Finish

Once your hip is flexed to 90 degrees, adduct your knee across your body. Once you have reached your end range of motion, return to the start position with the hip flexed, and repeat.

Tips and Progressions

Once you have mastered the rotation with a flexed knee, attempt the same movement but add a hip extension before you start the next rotation.

a

b

Training one leg at a time transfers strength gains to the sport environment, where movement is achieved one leg at a time. Incorporating the stability ball facilitates a deeper range of motion and also assists in the concentric positive phase back to a standing position. A DSL ball will stay in place so you can drop your glutes onto it.

Setup

Begin in a seated position, hips on the top front side of the DSL stability ball, centering one foot on the floor at the midline of your body. Sit up tall and set the core. The opposite foot is extended forward.

Movement

Lift up and extend the grounded leg to a standing position. Balance before returning, under control, to a seated position.

Tips and Progressions

- Use a controlled bounce to help initiate the concentric lift phase if you are unable to rise up to stand from a static seated position.
- Always double-check that the DSL stability ball is perfectly in place behind you for each rep.
- If one leg is not as strong, begin your first set with that leg and finish your last set with that leg—effectively completing one extra set for the weaker leg.

a   b

LEG–HIP–CORE MULTIDIRECTIONAL CONTROL

The purpose of this exercise is not to apply the greatest force, such as during a leg press. It is designed to challenge the inner unit to stabilize the supine position while the hips and legs adjust position.

Setup

Lie on the floor with your knees flexed. You and your partner together hold a stability ball between your feet. Increase the foot pressure on the ball to lift it up until the lower legs are parallel to the floor.

Movement

Cooperatively move the ball forward, backward, up, down, and sideways while keeping the back flat on the floor.

Tips and Progressions

Complete the same exercise with each partner using only one leg, as shown in the photo.

GOLDY'S LEG BLASTER

The inner and outer thighs are two areas that athletes have always had a difficult time training. Most exercises for these areas are completed with the foot off the floor (with the multihip machine or cable attachments). The problem with these exercises is that they don't transfer to actual sport situations. The inner and outer thigh muscles are most often used in movements that require the foot to be in contact with the floor. The leg blaster can train these muscles in this manner.

Setup

Set up close to an adjustable-cable column using a 45-centimeter ball. Place a cable belt around your inside ankle, with your foot sitting on top of the ball. The outside leg is your plant and should maintain a bent-knee position. Your hips are back, and your abdominals are set. This setup method emphasizes the inner thighs and quads.

Movement

To activate the inner-thigh muscles, the initial movement comes from the inside of the foot pressing down on the ball. Once you have established this pressure, roll the ball toward you by bringing your hip in. Maintain the natural curve in your lower back and keep the hips back.

Finish

Return to the starting position by releasing your leg, allowing it a full range of motion on the return.

Variation

You can also focus on the outer-thigh muscles by placing the cable on the opposite leg, as described previously. The movement and sequence are the same, but the main difference is that you push out instead of pull in.

a

b

HIP POWER INITIATION

Most athletes have imbalances in hip mobility caused by body structure (such as a difference in leg lengths) and repetitive actions specific to the mechanics of their sports. This exercise exposes imbalances while strengthening two key movements: inward and outward rotation. A goal is to isolate the hips from the trunk; you aim to keep the chest facing the floor and the shoulders square while the hips rotate. While the goal is to minimize trunk rotation, the hip power achieved through this exercise contributes to rotary power either from the top down (as in swinging a tennis racket) or from the ground up (as in pivoting to change direction).

Setup

Begin crouched behind the stability ball. Move on top of the ball and walk out with the hands until you are in a short-lever push-up position with the knees on the ball. Flex the knees to bring the feet up in the air. Hold the legs and feet together. Select a ball size that allows a level line from knee to shoulder.

Movement

Keeping the trunk and shoulders square to the floor, rotate at the hips—think of two pivot points, one on each side of the hips. Rotate the hips to place the ball and knees out to the side of the body. Return through to the opposite side of the body, alternating sides.

Tips and Progressions

- Begin with a slow tempo to safely build strength, stability, control, and range of motion.
- Once you've achieved all these and have them well trained over several workouts, you can vary the tempo, with a goal of fast movement. Rotate to the left and immediately reverse direction to the opposite side, where you pause at each rep. This focuses power initiation off one side. The eccentric–concentric coupling builds power initiation.
- You can also move at a higher pace with fluidity from side to side without pausing.

a

b

PRONE BALL HOLD WITH KNEE DRIVE

This exercise helps you build premovement core activation and trunk stability to hold a push-up position and stabilize yourself on the ball. It also works the lower abdominals and hip flexors when you add leg movement. Holding your body weight on the ball preloads the core for stabilization and movement. The best way to understand this is to experience it.

Setup

Assume a push-up position with the heels of the hands on the upper outside of the ball and fingers wrapped down the ball. Feet are on the floor, up on toes in a shoulder-width stance. With straight arms, sink into the middle back before flexing the elbows two inches (five centimeters). Load your body weight onto the arms and engage the core.

Movement

Slowly bring the knee of one leg straight up as close to the chest as possible, pause, and return. Switch legs, bringing the knee of the opposite leg in toward the chest, pause, and continue to alternate legs.

Middle Position

Progress by lengthening the pause in the middle position for each rep. If the longer hold results in a rounded back, return to regular fluid reps with no pause.

Tips and Progressions

- For an advanced progression that increases activation of the transverse abdominis and internal hip rotators, pull the knee in and over to the opposite elbow. Begin with a slow, controlled tempo along with a half-second pause at the middle position.
- To progress, first lengthen the pauses.
- Once you have built the strength to handle this, increase the speed of movement, driving the knee to the opposite elbow before holding.

a

b

LUNGE WITH MEDICINE BALL PASS

 This complex exercise takes an important leg strength exercise and adds upper-body power.

Setup

Partners face each other, about three to four strides apart. One partner has a medicine ball.

Movement

While holding the ball, lift one leg off the floor, flexing at the hip and knee, and cycle it forward to softly plant it on the floor ahead of the body. The lunge length is long enough to produce a 90-degree angle at the knee (your knee cannot go past your toes) and low enough that your thigh is parallel to the floor. Before landing, pass the ball toward your partner.

Finish

Hold the lunge position and focus to remain well balanced. While receiving the return pass, push off with your lead foot to return to the starting position.

Tips and Progressions

Lunge and catch: One partner lunges and catches while the other throws. Alternate lunging with the left and right leg while receiving passes at random. Your partner passes directly in front of you to a variety of places outside your midline and changes position to deliver passes across your body (passes sent from off to the side). The pass reception sequence is always catch, balance, and hold for two seconds before returning the ball to your partner and taking your next lunge step.

This exercise builds strength and dynamic flexibility in the legs, hips, and torso, which also links these muscles together.

Setup

Stand upright, holding a medicine ball just below chest height.

Movement

Lift the left leg off the floor, flexing at the hip and knee as in photo *a*, and cycle it forward to softly plant it on the floor ahead of the body. The lunge length is long enough to produce a 90-degree angle at the knee (your knee cannot position out past your toes) and low enough that your thigh is parallel to the floor. As you land, twist over to the forward-leg (left-leg) side.

Finish

Push off with the rear foot (right) to stand back upright, and continue forward with the right leg into a lunge position. As you land, rotate over to the right leg as in photo *b*. Continue for a set number of repetitions.

Tips and Progressions

Lunge and rotate with arms extended: Hold the ball as far away from your torso as possible. The longer the lever arm and the farther away the ball from your torso and center of gravity, the greater the load on your shoulders, back, and torso.

a   b

Develop stride strength, challenge single-leg balance, and improve muscle sequencing from toes to fingertips for more functional muscle recruitment when you blend legs, shoulders, and balance. The heavier the medicine ball, the more shoulder strength required.

Setup

Stand balanced on a single leg while holding a medicine ball in one hand at the shoulder on the same side as the support leg. Set and brace the core, and establish a strong middle back. Steady the ankle, and slightly flex the knee.

Movement

Cycle the free leg up and out in front of the body in as long a stride as possible. Land softly—heel first—rolling to the full foot as you shift your weight forward, keeping the medicine ball at the shoulder. Keeping the head up, chest lifted, and the abdominal muscles tight, slowly lower your hips toward the floor until the back knee is just above the floor and the lead knee is flexed to about 90 degrees with the upper leg parallel to the floor. If the front knee is ahead of that foot, spread the feet farther apart.

Middle Position

Shift body weight forward to the lead foot, and forcefully push off the floor by extending the front hip and knee. Let the effort come from the front leg to achieve a standing position as you press the medicine ball overhead. The back knee drives forward, finishing at waist height. From this single-leg balanced position with the arm remaining fully extended, lower the medicine ball laterally until the arm is parallel to the floor, pause slightly, then raise the medicine ball back up overhead. Pass it across to complete the same movements with the opposite arm.

Finish

Pass the ball back to your original arm, lower the medicine ball back to the shoulder, reach and step back into the lunge position, and drive off the lead leg back into a single-leg standing position.

Tips and Progressions

- To advance the challenge, visually track the medicine ball to the side. Begin tracking with just your eyes. Think of tunnel vision, where your eyes watch only the medicine ball.
- Advance to moving your entire head to follow the ball. Tilt your head to look up at the ball.
- You can also increase the weight of the medicine ball.

a b c

SPLIT STRIDE

This exercise works the musculature used for movement skills common to many sports: open steps, drop steps, and angled lunges. The emphasis is on strength but the exercise is designed to challenge dynamic flexibility through the hips, low back, and adductors.

Setup

Begin in a slight split position, with the front leg straight and rear leg flexed with the tip of the rear foot (toes) on top of the stability ball. Jump and shuffle your front foot to ensure the legs are split 2 feet (61 centimeters) apart. Engage the core and correct trunk positioning until you achieve a stable position.

Movement

Firing the postural muscles of the trunk, push the toes of your back foot into the ball as you extend and outwardly rotate the leg, rolling the ball back at a 45-degree angle. As you kick back the leg, the foot moves with the ball. Allow a longer stride by flexing the front leg to 90 degrees. Move your arms naturally as you would when running.

Middle Position

In the middle position your back leg is fully extended, pushed back and to the side, ending with a 45-degree angle. The inside of the foot meets the outside of the ball. The front leg is flexed to 90 degrees so that the tibia is perpendicular to the floor and the knee is not out past the toes. In the middle position, note the strong load on the front leg and flexibility demands through the hips and low back. In the middle stance, the opposite arm joins the front leg. Cue "Chest up" to keep the trunk upright, but allow *slight* forward flexion, which accommodates the stride stance.

Finish

Extend the front leg as you pull the ball back in toward the body, finishing in an upright position.

Tips and Progressions

- If flexibility limits the range of motion or forces excessive forward trunk flexion to accommodate a stride, switch to a smaller ball. Even for tall participants, often a 55-centimeter ball or even a 45-centimeter ball works better for lunge-type strength ball exercises, allowing full range of motion for strength until flexibility catches up.
- If you find that your front knee is pressured out past the toes or that the ball travels up your back leg, adjust the setup position to a longer split stance.

a   b

Most athletes have imbalances in hip mobility caused by body structure (such as a difference in leg lengths) and repetitive actions specific to the mechanics of their sports. This exercise exposes imbalances while strengthening two key movements: inward and outward rotation. A goal is to isolate the hips from the trunk; you aim to keep the chest facing the floor and the shoulders square while the hips rotate. The improved hip strength contributes to rotary power, lateral deceleration, and stride movement patterns.

Setup

Begin crouched behind the stability ball. Move on top of the ball and walk out with your hands until you are in a prone push-up position with feet on the ball. Release one foot.

Movement

Move the knee of the free leg down and around the body as the leg on the ball rotates to the inside. Unwind this movement and continue past neutral (setup) position, moving the free leg up and over the body. The goal is to touch the foot to the floor on the opposite side of the body.

Finish

Return back to the prone setup position. Adjust the foot on the ball if necessary before entering the next repetition.

Tips and Progressions

- This exercise looks complex, but it is very achievable. In the learning stage, it is easy for the leg to fall off the ball during rotation. Practice with a spotter behind the ball whose hands will "bookend" the ball, allowing the ball to travel only an inch (about 2.5 centimeters) in either direction.

- In your workout, make sure this exercise does not follow a tough chest-push set; otherwise it will be difficult to hold the setup position for the desired rep count.

a

b

KNEELING SIDE PASS

This exercise works the hips and torso with a frontal plane loading through side flexion of the trunk.

Setup

Partners stand 4 feet (1.2 meters) apart, both facing the same wall. One partner has a medicine ball. Begin in a kneeling position with the torso upright.

Movement

Partner A passes to partner B. Partner B catches the ball above head height, about an inch (2.5 centimeters) in front of the body. Absorb the catch and follow through as far as possible to the opposite side while keeping the torso upright.

Finish

Partner B brings the ball back overhead and follows through with a side-overhead pass back to partner A.

Tips and Progressions

Standing catch: Position the feet shoulder-width apart. Flex the knees and set the abdominals. Turn the head to see your partner. Catch the ball above head height and about an inch in front of your body, but follow through farther to the opposite side. If accuracy allows, move farther apart to require more power on the throw and more load on the catch reception.

a

b

This is a great full-body exercise. You will feel this in the legs, back, core, and shoulders.

Setup

Stand with feet at shoulder width. Hold a medicine ball with two hands in front of the body.

Movement

Step out to the left and lower into a lateral squat position, shifting body weight over the left leg. As you lower over the left leg, push the medicine ball out away from your chest until arms are fully extended. Hold this position for two seconds.

Finish

Push off the left leg to move back into a neutral stance. As you push off the left leg, pull the ball back in toward your chest. Next, step out to the right, and extend your arms to push the ball out away from your chest and lower into a side squat position. Hold for two seconds. Push off the right leg and pull the ball back in to return to the start position.

a   b

SQUAT PRESS

This exercise combines a squat and sit-up with arms fully extended under load. Use a DSL stability ball to safely execute the movement pattern while holding dumbbells.

Setup

Set your DSL stability ball in neutral ball position (label up). The DSL stability ball has circle markings that can be used as a reference point in an effort to complete the supine portion without ball movement and to define a target spot to aim for that will help you avoid falling off the ball.

Begin in a standing position in front of the DSL stability ball. Feet are shoulder-width apart, core is set and braced, and middle back is set. Hold light dumbbells above your head (in a shoulder press position), arms extended.

Movement

Maintaining solid posture, squat by lowering the hips into a seated position so that the glutes touch at about the outer edge of the large top circle. Sit down on the top front side of your DSL stability ball, keeping the arms extended overhead. Lie back into a bridge position, arms still extended, now up over the chest.

Finish

Sit up off the DSL ball, shifting the arms overhead so that you stand up with arms extended overhead.

Tips and Progressions

- Learn this exercise with *no* dumbbells but assume the same arm position.
- Next, begin with the lightest weight and progress step by step. The load you can handle will be limited by strength, stability, and flexibility in the shoulders and back.

a

b

c

Chest

Exercises in This Chapter

The incline dumbbell press focuses on the upper pectoral muscles. This exercise is typically performed on an incline bench, but you can perform it on a ball to incorporate the elements of balance and stability to the upper extremity.

Setup

In this exercise a larger ball is necessary for the correct support. Holding dumbbells, sit on a ball, and slowly walk out to a position in which your head, shoulders, and back are supported by the ball. Ensure that your feet are slightly wider than hip width to provide a safe initial base of support.

Movement

Begin by setting your abdominals and pressing your arms in an upward arc to the point where your hands are over your eyes.

Finish

Once you have reached the top position, return the dumbbells to a point where they touch the tops of your shoulders.

Tips and Progressions

You can increase the difficulty of this exercise by using the following methods:

- Decrease the width of your feet to increase the stability factor for this exercise.
- Perform a one-arm dumbbell press to greatly increase the difficulty of this exercise; this will require greater core stabilization.

Safety Notes

Ensure that the floor is clean and dust free. As you press into the ball on an angle, a clean and dust-free floor will help in preventing the ball from rolling out and away from you.

Hand Position

The hand position shown is the traditional grip. A neutral grip, in which the palms face each other, places the shoulders under less stress than the traditional bench press position. In the traditional position the palms face away and the shoulders are externally rotated. If you have any kind of shoulder ailment, you should use the neutral grip position.

ONE-ARM DUMBBELL PRESS

This exercise integrates anterior deltoids, pectorals, and core stabilization with a unilateral lift.

Setup

Sit on the stability ball with a dumbbell in one hand. Walk out so that you are in a supine position with your head and shoulders supported on the ball and feet at shoulder-width stance. Activate the core and glutes to keep the hips up and stable on the ball. Start with the entire dumbbell outside the shoulder.

Movement

The concentric movement will begin similar to a bench press action: Push the weight up on an arc, finishing above the shoulder.

Middle Position

In mid-rep, the arm is fully extended. Maintain a strong supine bridge with the glutes firing to keep the hips up level with knees and trunk. Shoulders remain on top of the ball.

Finish

Slowly lower the dumbbell under control, out and down, back to the setup position outside the shoulder. Bringing the load outside the midline will accelerate the demands for the core to stabilize the body position.

Tips and Progressions

- To progress, alternately increase the weight and decrease the base of support by bringing the feet closer together. Decreasing the base of support increases core activation while increasing the weight on the pecs and shoulders.
- If prime mover strength is your goal, to integrate some instability but prioritize the load imposed on the muscles, set up with a DSL stability ball and use a wide base of support, which allows you to use a heavier dumbbell.

The dumbbell press is more of a general chest movement that focuses on the whole pectoral area.

Setup

Holding dumbbells, sit on a ball and slowly walk out to a position in which your head and shoulders are supported by the ball. Your feet are slightly wider than hip width to provide a safe initial base of support.

Movement

Begin by setting your abdominals and pressing your arms in an upward arc to the point where your hands are over your eyes.

Finish

Once you have reached the top position, return the dumbbells to a point where they touch the tops of your shoulders.

a

b

This exercise takes the old dumbbell bench press and turns it into something much more functional for shoulder and core development. Although this has been designated as a chest exercise, significant core rotation is demonstrated here.

Setup

Begin by holding a single dumbbell in your right hand and sitting on a stability ball. Walk out so that you are in the tabletop position with your head and shoulders supported by the ball. Activate your core and especially your glutes. The right arm is set in the bottom position of a dumbbell press.

Movement

From the bottom position, drive the dumbbell up and toward the midline of the body, as you would in a standard dumbbell bench press.

Finish

Just as you are about to reach full extension of your arm, rotate your body and continue to drive the weight. The momentum will cause you to roll to your left, and you will end up being supported by your left arm.

a

b

155

SUPINE DUMBBELL PRESS AND FLY

 This exercise provides a great challenge to the pectorals because it combines two popular movements for the chest. The supine dumbbell press and fly also requires great coordination.

Setup

With dumbbells in each hand, sit on a stability ball and roll out so you are in a tabletop position. One arm is in a flexed position, or the bottom position of a dumbbell bench press. The other arm is in a position similar to the bottom position of a dumbbell fly with a slight bend in the elbow. Glutes and core are activated to provide a stable base for movement.

Movement

The concentric movement begins with the bench press arm and the fly arm initiating movement at the same time. The fly-arm angle at the elbow should not change during the lifting.

Finish

Both dumbbells meet over the top of the chest. The press-side arm supinates as you reach the top. This results in internal rotation at the shoulder, which will assist in a more effective contraction of the pectoralis major. Complete your set on one side and then switch arm positions.

Tips and Progressions

- By changing your hand position on the dumbbells, you can target different parts of your pectoral muscle. Try varying your grip from prone to supine to neutral.
- You can add a weight vest or sandbag over your abdominals to increase the activity of the core and glutes.

The cable fly provides excellent recruitment of your whole pec muscle. Additionally, as a result of the single-arm movement, there is a great demand on your core musculature to stabilize yourself on the ball.

Setup

Place the stability ball beside a low pulley with a single handle attached to the cable. Taking hold of the handle, sit on the ball and roll forward until you are in a supine extended position. Your hips and back should be parallel to the floor.

Movement

Your arm is in the low position with your elbow slightly bent, which will alleviate any stress at this joint. Movement should be in a horizontal plane, across your body. The lower you pull your arm across, the more activation the sternal portion of your pec will receive. The higher you pull, the greater the activation of the clavicular part of your pec.

Finish

Once you have moved your arm through your own range, hold the end position for a second and return to the initial position.

a

b

This is the perfect replacement for the pec deck. Not only do you work your chest in a very demanding exercise, but you also work your entire body as you attempt to maintain proper posture.

Setup

Use two stability balls by bringing both balls together, side by side. Place each of your lower arms on a ball. Your body is on a 45-degree angle, with normal curvature of your low back.

Movement

Begin movement by rolling the balls outward and allowing your arms to open up. Move to a point where you feel you have reached a comfortable range of motion. If you have any kind of shoulder problem, you should avoid this exercise because it places great stress on the anterior capsule of the shoulder.

Finish

Once you have reached the range of motion that you are comfortable with, squeeze your arms back together, bringing the balls back to the start position.

a

b

STANDING TWO-BALL ROLLOUT

This exercise places the body in a closed kinetic chain athletic stance. An aggressive abdominal and low back exercise, the standing two-ball rollout also requires contribution from all major muscle groups in the entire body, from foot to fingertip, an ultimate linked system. This also develops the entire shoulder girdle.

Setup

Stand in front of two balls positioned side by side. Move into a pelvic tilt, moving your glutes forward and drawing in your navel toward your spine. Keeping your torso upright, flex at your knees and drop your hips into a balanced athletic stance. Place one hand on top of each ball, and shift some of your weight onto your hands. The load should be distributed equally between your legs, upper body, and core.

Movement

Keeping your hands in place, pivot on your toes as you roll the balls away from your body. To maintain an equal split of the load throughout your body, drop your hips as the ball rolls away from your knees. Roll out to as long a lever as you can safely handle. If you feel any strain in your low back, make sure you are not in the superman pose. If your back discomfort remains, return to the setup stage and check your pelvic tilt.

Finish

Hold at the far reach for two seconds and then roll back in to the starting position.

Tips and Progressions

Alternating rolls: Follow the same setup instructions. Then, keeping your hands in place, pivot on your toes as you roll the balls away from your body. Shift your weight up and over the balls so you are in more of a push-up position on top of the balls. This is your starting position. Holding your feet, legs, and hips in place, simultaneously roll one ball back in toward your body and the other ball farther away. Continue in this pattern for the designated reps.

a

b

This exercise challenges the upper-body musculature while requiring core strength and stabilization. This is an excellent shoulder stabilization exercise that works the posterior deltoids.

Setup

Standing behind the ball, crouch down and place your abdominals on top of the ball. Roll forward until your hands reach the floor in front of the ball. Walk your hands out until your hips are off the ball and your quadriceps rest on top of the ball.

Movement

Focus on maintaining a strong core by contracting the postural muscles to keep the hips up strong and the body aligned. (Prevent hips from sagging, and avoid any hip or torso rotation.) Walk your hands out until your feet remain on top of the ball.

Finish

Do one push-up and then walk the hands back in toward the ball until your hips are once again on top of the ball. Pay close attention to the movement of your shoulder blades. If you have a winging or protruding shoulder blade as you lower yourself, you should avoid this exercise and seek medical advice.

Tips and Progressions

- When you complete the push-up, hold only one foot on top of the ball. The other leg is removed at the far position of each rep and held straight.
- Walk out as fast as you can, then to return back to the ball, jump with both hands together in a plyometric action, and shuffle back to the setup position.
- Walk out as slowly as you can, supporting yourself on only one hand for an extended time. Keep your hips up strong and aligned without hip or torso rotation; your shoulders and hips should face square to the floor.

a

b

JUMP-OUT TO PUSH-UP

 This is a dynamic upper-body plyometric exercise for training power. Most people are used to the feeling of jumping in the legs. The same abilities are needed in the upper body to fuel sport skills and avoid injury when absorbing falls. It uses a deceleration–acceleration coupling through the eccentric (landing and braking) and concentric (jumping) phases. You should be competent in doing push-ups and also capable of completing sets of walk-out push-ups before progressing to this exercise.

Setup

Begin crouched behind the stability ball. Roll onto the ball, extend the arms in front of the body, and set the core and middle back.

Movement

Roll right over the ball until the hands reach the floor. Absorb the landing and immediately extend the arms with enough power to release the hands from the floor.

Aim each subsequent landing a little farther away from the ball, carrying the body out to a full push-up position with the feet on the ball. Jump with the hands back in toward the ball all the way to the crouched setup position.

Tips and Progressions

- When first trying this exercise, try to land softly and move through each partial push-up fluidly before releasing the hands in the air.
- If you are ready to try the exercise but do not have much strength, you can minimize elbow flexion on the landing and minimize jump height. Just unload body weight from the hands. This results in a jump-shuffling of the hands out away from the ball.

a

b

165

This exercise develops braking and absorbing abilities that benefit powerful sport mechanics. The eccentric loading on an unstable surface improves muscle strength and reactivity in the core, shoulders, and posterior chain. Complete sets with the simplest demands and then progress to more difficult versions one step at a time. You must be able to complete multiple sets of ball balance push-ups and floor push-ups (feet on ball) before progressing to jump push-ups.

Setup

Prepare for the exercise by assuming a push-up position with feet on the floor shoulder-width apart and hands on the ball. The heel of the hand should rest on the outside upper portion of the ball with the fingers wrapped down around the ball. Set your core, load through the scapula, and press (squeeze) into the ball.

Movement

While remaining strong through the trunk and hips, lower the chest to the top of the ball, then extend the arms to push your body mass back to the top position. Push up with enough exertion to travel past the setup position, unloading your body mass from the ball.

Middle Position

At the middle position, land back onto the ball, catching your mass with good hand placement and slight elbow flexion. Try to brake and stop the movement as soon as possible.

Finish

After you land, catch, brake, and pause, resume lowering into another rep.

Tips and Progressions

- Spend extra time preparing for the exercise, ensuring you have set the core and upper back and have optimal body positioning, hand placement, and foot width.

- If you are new to this exercise, starting with a DSL ball will add stability to the landing.

- Spend time training at the following levels before advancing further:
  1. Push up to unload your body mass from the ball, releasing the heel of the hands but keeping fingers securely positioned on the ball. This provides the dynamic eccentric loading but reduces the load, skill, and balance required. Most active strength training enthusiasts can safely handle this level.
  2. Push off the ball until the full hand releases, producing as little height as possible.
  3. Push off higher, progressing the height over a number of workouts.

4. Add to the push-off jump height by also pulling the hands toward the trunk, maximizing the coordination and strength needed for absorbing the eccentric loading.
5. Revert to level 1 or 2 but land and catch with one hand only. Roll to two hands for the lowering and push-up phase, alternating arms on the catch.

a

b

This exercise not only works the chest area of the shoulder but also ties in the significant requirement of core stabilization.

Setup

Stand approximately three to four feet (about a meter) from a wall. Place a medicine ball about 4 inches (10 centimeters) below the line from your shoulder, and hold the ball with an extended arm against the wall. You will need to be on your toes with your core engaged as you lean into the ball with your one arm. Do not allow any rotation in the core as you get into the setup position.

Movement

While maintaining stabilization of your core, eccentrically lower your body toward the wall. You must do this in a slow and controlled manner.

Finish

Once you have lowered yourself down to a point where your shoulder is almost in full extension, press back out, again in a controlled manner. This movement is not meant to be performed with a fast tempo.

Tips and Progressions

- To increase the difficulty of this exercise, decrease the base of support by using a smaller medicine ball.
- Try unilateral leg support by raising the leg opposite of the working arm.

BALL WALK-AROUND

This is a great exercise for shoulder stabilization and core stability. The purpose is to load each shoulder independently.

Setup

Standing behind the ball, crouch down and place your abdominals on top of the ball. Roll forward until your hands reach the floor in front of the ball. Walk your hands out until your hips are off the ball. Continue to walk your hands out away from the ball until only your feet remain on the ball.

Movement

At this point, focus on maintaining a strong core and contracting the postural muscles to keep the hips up strong and body aligned. (Prevent the hips from sagging, and avoid any hip or torso rotation.) Maintaining a long lever (feet on the ball with body in a push-up position), walk your hands laterally to rotate your body around the ball in a clockwise direction. Pick up your right hand and move it away from your midline, supporting your body weight with your left arm until you replant the right hand. Next, pick up your left hand and move it in closer to the right hand. Alternate these steps so your hands complete a circle around the ball. Maintain a strong body alignment as you move your hands.

Finish

The movement is finished once you complete a 360-degree circle. Next, complete this pattern in a counterclockwise direction.

a

b

171

MEDICINE BALL CHEST PASS

Chest passes link strength and power in the chest, shoulder, and back. The catch is absorbed with the core and legs. The return pass is initiated from the legs and hips and completed with the chest and arms. In its advanced form, it is an excellent full-body multijoint exercise.

Setup

Stand facing your partner, about three paces apart. Keep your feet shoulder-width apart, knees slightly flexed, and abdominals precontracted. Both participants set up with the arms fully extended out level with the chest. The hands are open, making a definitive target.

Movement

Partner A draws the ball into the chest and reverses direction to push the ball out away from the body and onto partner B. Partner B first makes ball contact with the arms fully extended. The ball is sequentially absorbed through flexing of the arms and knees to cushion the catch. Partner B tries to overcome the eccentric loading as quickly as possible, immediately reversing direction to push the ball back toward partner A.

Finish

When you pass, after releasing the ball, keep your arms extended and up and out away from the chest, with an open hand target. Continue this sequence for a set number of repetitions.

Tips and Progressions

- For speed, complete the same exercise technique but position only two paces apart. Pass as quickly as possible, trying to eliminate any pause at the chest between the negative and positive phases of movement. Hand targets are important for protecting your face. Be positioned to maintain the rapid pass succession.

- For strength, repeat the same exercise instruction, but five paces apart. Minimize the time between the negative phase and reverse direction into a positive push phase. This will be more challenging because the load you catch will be heavier with the extra distance. More full-body linked strength is needed for propelling the ball the required distance.

STANDING PARTNER STABILITY BALL CHEST PRESS

This exercise upgrades a push movement pattern into a closed kinetic chain position. Working with a partner, it begins with a focus on the eccentric phase linked with shoulder and core stabilization. Following this preparatory work, it advances to a whole-body, multijoint push action.

Setup

Partners stand facing one another with the core braced, middle back set, feet shoulder-width apart. The "braking and stabilizing" partner begins with arms fully extended; the "pushing" partner starts with arms flexed and ball at the chest.

Movement

One partner extends the arms to push the ball forward while the other slows the movement down, actively braking the force. Brace strongly to anchor the torso during the standing push. Likewise, maintain a set middle back so you do not compensate through the shoulders.

Finish

Once the ball is pushed through to the partner's chest, reverse roles and continue back and forth, alternating between pushing and braking.

Tips and Progressions

- Anyone with arms fully extended has the benefit of a locked lever system that is stronger than most muscular force. So to allow the partner to initiate the first rep, the braking and stabilizing partner may have to slightly flex at the elbows. To accommodate partners of unequal strength, the braking and stabilizing partner can ease up to allow the pushing partner to successfully extend the arms to a full range-of-motion push.

- After working on the exercise through several workouts and demonstrating solid posture and shoulder position during the braking action, advance to a multijoint push. In this version, before pushing, drop your center of mass by loading up the legs into a partial squat position. Focus on the sequential firing of muscles through the legs, hips, chest, and arms to first drive from the legs then push from the chest. This will require greater strength from the braking partner, who may now have to adopt a split stance position to provide enough resistance.

a

b

This exercise works on dynamic strength, eccentric absorption, and joint stabilization in a standing position, improving the transferability into real-life and sport demands.

Setup

Partners stand facing one another, core braced, middle back set, feet shoulder-width apart. Hold two stability balls, each partner pressing into the ball to hold it in place. Flex the knees to anchor into an athletic-ready stance, but keep the trunk upright (as opposed to leaning into the partner) to place more emphasis on trunk stability and back musculature.

Movement

Partners simultaneously extend one arm to push a ball forward while using the opposite arm to resist the partner's push. Before the exercise, define whether you want to aim to hold the trunk in a neutral posture position or if you prefer to allow some rotation to assist the concentric push and eccentric braking through a functional range of motion. Both have benefits.

Tips and Progressions

Once you can complete this exercise with good technique and control, and after you've completed several workouts to train strength and stabilization, increase the speed to more explosive, rapid pushes. On the resisting arm, you will need to harness more leg, gluteal, trunk, middle back, and shoulder strength to resist and absorb the pushed ball while stabilizing the entire body within the base of support.

PUSH-UP PASS

This is a great upper-body plyometric exercise that prepares the body for eccentric loading and concentric power.

Setup

Partners are two strides apart, both kneeling on the back edge of a sit-up mat so the rest of the mat is out in front of their bodies. Torso is upright. One partner has a medicine ball.

Movement

Partner A (who has the ball) begins the drill by passing chest to chest to his partner. The arms remain extended out and the torso follows the pass, falling forward until the hands make contact on the sit-up mat and absorb the body into a push-up position. Powerfully push back up to reverse the direction and propel the torso back up into a kneeling position. On the way back up, as soon as both partners make eye contact, partner B returns the pass back to partner A and falls into a push-up position.

Finish

Continue this sequence for a set number of reps or until fatigue prevents pushing back up to a kneeling position. Especially as you fatigue and the tempo slows and decision making becomes inhibited, remember to wait for eye contact before returning passes.

a

b

STANDING–LYING PARTNER PUSH-UP AND PRESS

 This exercise develops less power than the standing partner chest press but is excellent for strength and joint stability. It capitalizes on the muscle reactivity needed for accommodating the shifting ball as the partner tries to hold it.

Setup

Partner A lies faceup on the floor with knees flexed, feet flat on the floor, and core set. Partner B stands up in front of partner A's feet. Facing each other, they hold a stability ball between them with the heels of their hands on the ball and fingers wrapping down around the sides of the ball. Elbows are only slightly flexed. Partner B stands with flexed knees, weight leaning into the ball.

Movement

Partner A flexes the arms to slowly lower the ball (and partial weight of partner) to the chest before pressing back up. During this movement, partner B pivots on the toes to travel with the ball as it is lowered. The goal for partner B is to stabilize on the ball, maintaining a straight line from heel to shoulder.

Partner A next presses into the ball, extending the arms to push the ball back up (against partner B's body weight). This relies on partner B to isometrically contract to hold the ball in place during the movement.

Finish

After partner A pushes the ball back up to the setup position, partner B lowers into the ball and then pushes back up, relying on partner A to isometrically contract to hold the ball in place.

Tips and Progressions

- Give each partner sets in both positions.
- An advanced challenge is for partner A to slightly shift the ball left and right during his push-up, challenging partner B to maintain a locked system from heel to trunk while the ball is being lowered and raised.

Shoulders and Upper Back

Exercises in This Chapter

PRONE ROW EXTERNAL ROTATION

The goal of the prone row external rotation is to integrate two functional movements into one exercise. Recruitment of the extensor muscles of the entire spine is also emphasized during this exercise.

Setup

Place the stability ball under your middle chest and align your body so that your knees, hips, shoulders, and neck are in a neutral aligned position as demonstrated in the setup position.

Movement

With your hands holding dumbbells in an extended position under the shoulders, pull your elbows directly up, ensuring that your upper arms are in a straight line across your body. If you were viewing this from the top, you could draw a straight line from elbow to elbow, right across the upper back. The elbows should never rise above this horizontal line. If you have problems with shoulder impingement, you should find a comfortable range of motion slightly below this position to ease any potential shoulder pain.

Finish

Once you bring your elbows up, stabilize this position and externally rotate your upper arms. Maintain a 90-degree angle at the elbow joint, which will guarantee a longer lever and ensure optimal loading of the external rotator musculature. Rotate to the point where your upper and lower arm are in a horizontal position with the floor, as demonstrated in the finish position. Hold this position for one second and then derotate. Lower arms to the start position and repeat for a set number of reps.

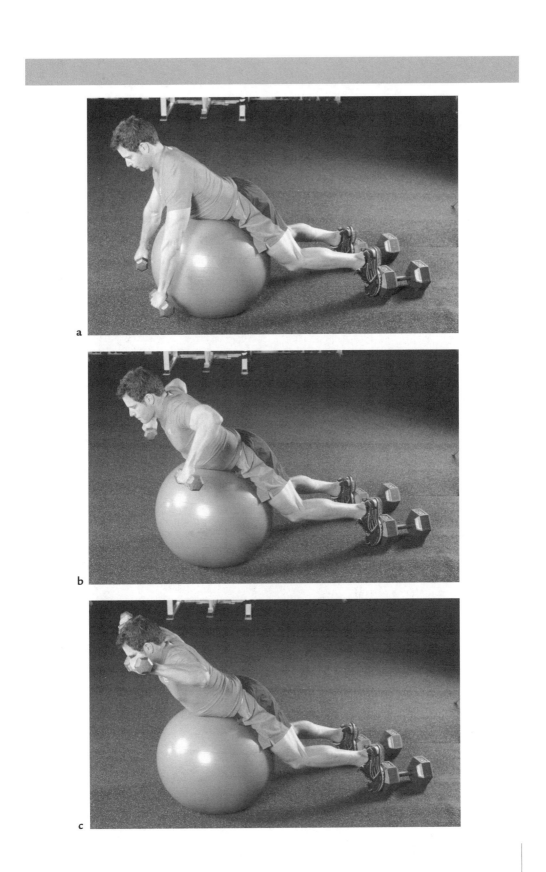

a

b

c

CROSS-BODY REAR DELT RAISE

This exercise targets the important muscles in the back of the shoulders that help to stabilize the shoulder blades. The position in which you place your body will also challenge your core muscles.

Setup

Lie sideways over the ball, with the ball placed in your armpit and on the side of your chest. Maintain this lateral position throughout the movement.

Movement

Set your abdominals and draw in your navel. With your arm extended and pointing toward the floor holding a dumbbell, begin to raise your arm away from your body.

Finish

As you continue to raise your arm, your core will be challenged to stabilize your body on the ball. Continue to maintain a good position on the ball. Bring your arm up to the point where it is 5 degrees before perpendicular. At this point, hold the position for two seconds, and lower the arm to the setup position for your next rep.

a

b

ISODYNAMIC REAR DELT RAISE

This is unique because it incorporates isometric exercise (muscle contraction with no movement) and movement all within a single exercise. The targeted muscles surround the shoulder, shoulder blade, neck extensors, and spinal extensors.

Setup

Lie prone on the ball, with the ball placed just below your chest. Your body should be positioned so that the ankles, knees, and hips are in line and the torso is flexed forward so your upper body is at about a 45-degree angle with the floor. With a dumbbell in each hand and while maintaining the setup position, raise your arms until they are almost parallel to the floor.

Movement

Once your arms are in the proper position, there is actually no movement. This is the isometric type of contraction. Hold this position for 5 to 10 seconds. Maintain good head posture during this effort.

Finish

After 5 to 10 seconds, you will find that the shoulder musculature tires quite quickly. To ease the load, change the angle at which the load is placed on your shoulders. Bend your knees and roll back on the ball approximately 20 degrees. Maintain the same posture and arm position. Once you have rolled back, you will be able to hold position for another 5 to 10 seconds. The set is now completed. Lower the dumbbells to the floor, and rest for the prescribed time.

The reverse fly stresses the shoulder through a large range of motion. The single-arm cross-body line of pull challenges the core to stabilize trunk and ball position.

Setup

Sitting on the stability ball, walk the feet out away from the ball until you achieve a supine bridge position: head and shoulder blades on the ball, back and hips parallel to the floor. Attach one end of the tubing to something solid such as a door frame or piece of exercise equipment. Hold the other handle of strength tubing across the body, with a prestretch on the strength tubing.

Movement

Keeping the elbow slightly flexed, pull the handle up and over your body in an arc.

Middle Position

In mid-rep, hips are up and trunk remains strong. With light tubing, the handle should end up level with the shoulder. With stronger resistance, stop above the shoulder for an isometric hold.

Finish

Bring the handle back over the body with a controlled pace, providing active resistance against the shortening tubing.

Tips and Progressions

- To regress, select lighter tubing or position the ball closer to where the other end of the strength tubing is fixed, but be sure to have a prestretch on the tubing at the setup position.
- Progress the drill with stronger tubing and slower movement on both the concentric (positive) and eccentric (negative) phases.
- For greater emphasis on shoulder strength, use heavier tubing and a wider base of support at the feet.
- For more core emphasis, use moderate tubing with a narrow base of support.

a

b

PULLOVER

The pullover is an excellent move that will help anyone who lacks overhead shoulder extension. This exercise takes your pectoral muscles and latissimus dorsi through a complete range of motion.

Setup

With a dumbbell in each hand, sit on a stability ball and roll out so you are in a table-top position. The ball should support your head and shoulders. Extend both arms so that your biceps are in line with your ears.

Movement

Flex your arms forward to a position where they are straight up at a 90-degree angle with your body.

Finish

Lower your arms back to the starting position and repeat.

Tips and Progressions

- Keep your core engaged and do not arch your back as you lower your arms down to the extended position.
- You can also alternate arms so that each one moves independently.

a

b

SUPINE LAT PULL AND DELT RAISE

This exercise focuses on training the contralateral muscles, which involves training the latissimus dorsi on the posterior side of one shoulder while training the anterior deltoid on the opposite shoulder.

Setup

With a dumbbell in each hand, sit on a stability ball and roll out so you are in a tabletop position. One arm should be in extension—the upper arm is in line with the ear—and the other arm is in a neutral position by the hip. Use a neutral grip. Activate the glutes and core to provide a stable base for movement.

Movement

Begin by flexing the extended arm; at the same time extend the opposite side. Both arms begin the movement in unison. Keep the glutes and core activated to maintain a stable base for movement.

Finish

Your arms will be in the opposite position to that of the starting position.

Tips and Progressions

- By changing your hand position from a neutral grip to palms facing the ceiling, you place a greater challenge on the latissimus dorsi in the overhead position. This is a result of the internal rotation at the shoulder that will change the grip. The lats are also an internal rotator.

- To increase the activity of the core and glutes, you can place a weight vest or sandbag over the abdominals.

PRONE FRONT RAISE LATERAL FLY

 The prone front raise lateral fly fires up your whole posterior chain with a major emphasis on the shoulder adductors and extensors. Coordination between the left and right sides of the body will be put to the test.

Setup

Depending on your type of floor, it may be advantageous to set up near a wall. Brace both feet against the base of the floor and wall while placing the stability ball just above your navel. Your head, shoulders, hips, and knees should form a fairly straight line at approximately 45 degrees. Holding dumbbells in both hands, your arms should be extended under your chest.

Movement

Engage your core before the shoulders fire. The left arm begins extending out to the side as a lateral fly, challenging your rhomboids and posterior deltoid. Bring this arm up to the point where it is in line with your body and parallel to the floor. You should be able to draw a line across your back, connecting your scapula with your elbow. At the same time your right arm will flex forward as you fire your anterior deltoid. This arm should flex forward to the point where it is in line with your head and parallel to the floor.

Finish

Once you have reached the contracted positions, hold them for a second or two. This will result in a stability and balance effort of your upper torso. After you pause, return to the starting position and reverse the movement. Now the left arm will flex forward and the right arm will extend out to the side.

SUPINE PULL-UP

 The supine pull-up is a great overall exercise for all muscles on the back side of the body. It requires postural muscles to fire to keep the body in proper alignment while the shoulders pull the body up and down.

Setup

Set yourself up in a power rack so that the height of the barbell will allow for full extension of your arms, without allowing your upper back to touch the floor. Your grip determines which muscles will be emphasized. An overhand grip with your elbows pointing outward directs more resistance to the posterior deltoid and rhomboids. An underhand grip with your elbows pointing inward emphasizes the latissimus dorsi. The grip should be shoulder width or slightly narrower for the underhand grip.

Begin with the ball under the knees. As you become stronger, you will progress by moving the ball toward your heels.

The size of your ball will dictate how hard the exercise will be. Begin with a smaller ball; as you become stronger, progress to a larger ball.

Movement

Before you begin to pull yourself up, ensure that your knees, hips, and shoulders are in line. The muscles in your hips and back should be precontracted to stabilize your body into this position. Avoid tucking your chin in to view your body. You should be looking at the ceiling, with your head in a neutral position.

As you begin your movement, pull yourself up to the point where you can touch your chest to the bar. As you reach this position, attempt to squeeze your shoulder blades together to emphasize the muscles between your shoulder blades and spine.

Finish

As your chest touches the bar, hold this position for two seconds, and lower yourself to the start position. Allow yourself to get a good stretch in your upper back, then repeat.

With so many great push exercises and lateral shoulder moves, special attention is required for the posterior chain. You enjoy the most versatile range of motion in the shoulder joint, but to balance out shoulder mobility, strength is needed. Rotator cuff exercises will help build a stronger shoulder base, equalizing the push and lateral strength. Strengthening the rotator cuff muscle group will also improve your ability to set the middle back by using force closure to anchor the shoulders before any strength maneuver.

Setup

Sit on the stability ball facing the strength tubing axis point, which you affix at floor level around a column or at home with a door attachment. Brace the core and set the upper back. Sit up tall on the ball with good posture and feet shoulder-width apart on the floor. Knees should be level or just below hip height. Holding the tubing or cable, your arm is in an abducted position with a 90-degree bend in the elbow.

Movement

Keeping the elbow up, pull the strength tubing up and back until the elbow is in line with and level to the shoulder. Keep pulling the tubing by rotating around the elbow. The elbow remains fixed while the hand moves up and over the elbow.

Middle Position

In mid-rep, your elbow remains level with the shoulder, hand above the shoulder, and trunk perpendicular to the line of pull.

Finish

Slowly lower the tubing under control, reversing the two movement phases. Rotate around the elbow until the hand is level with the elbow and shoulder, then release and extend the arm under control.

Tips and Progressions

- A common error is trunk rotation to assist the pull. If the trunk does not stay square to the line of pull, remove the ball and practice this exercise in a standing position (on the floor), or select lighter tubing that the rotator cuff muscles can handle without assistance from the trunk.
- To increase the complexity and core activation, perform the exercise while kneeling on the ball.

a

b

Two important muscles in the shoulder are the subscapularis and the serratus anterior. These muscles keep the shoulder blade against the rib cage during pressing movements. Scapular push-ups are an effective method of working this area.

Setup

Standing behind the ball, place your hands on the ball at shoulder width. Shuffle your feet back until your chest is over the ball and you are supported on your toes.

Movement

The movement is similar to that of regular push-ups. The difference is that the elbows do not flex and extend. All movement comes from a pushing movement out of the shoulder. This pushing movement creates a hunchback shape.

Finish

After pushing up to the point where you cannot push anymore, slowly lower yourself and allow your shoulder blades to come together without bending your elbows.

MEDICINE BALL SHOULDER STABILITY CIRCLE

 In many activities the shoulder is required to complete multiple duties such as stabilizing in one plane and moving in another, such as you would see in a contact sport when the arms are extended in a blocking pattern to keep an opponent away. At the same time you might experience contact from your side. This drill challenges the body in two ways: The static push component of the drill provides a need for stability in the sagittal plane, while the minicircles provide a multiplanar challenge to the shoulder. This is an excellent movement if you are rehabilitating the shoulder.

Setup

Begin by placing a medicine ball against the wall at shoulder height. Your feet are hip-width apart, and your body is in a solid athletic position. The arm is fully extended and parallel to the floor.

Movement

Press the ball into the wall so there is enough pressure to keep it in position. Once locked in this position, begin to make circles in a clockwise fashion.

Finish

After completing four to eight circles in a clockwise direction, reverse the movement and complete four to eight circles in a counterclockwise direction. Complete sets using both shoulders.

Tips and Progressions

- You can increase the difficulty of this drill by increasing the weight of your medicine ball.
- You can also increase the size of your circles to increase difficulty.

Whereas the standard push-up is an excellent chest developer, the pike push-up will drive more of the recruitment to the deltoids, as in a military press.

Setup

Begin with the ball under your belly and hands on the floor in a push-up position. Walk your hands forward so the ball begins to roll toward your feet. Toward the end of the walking, begin to contract your abdominals and flex at your hips. You will look like an inverted L. Holding this position, you are now ready to begin the movement.

Movement

Maintain a solid core, and flex at the elbows to slowly lower yourself to the point where your head is almost touching the floor.

Finish

Press yourself back up to the starting position and repeat.

Tips and Progressions

- To progress with the pike push-up, you can use more of a dynamic pike with each repetition. After each press, lower your legs back to a complete prone position with the ball under your feet, then pike back up to complete the next press.
- You can add a weight vest to increase the resistance.

The ability of your muscles to fire very powerfully and quickly will result in greater protection of your joints. This exercise trains the muscles of the shoulder joint to react very quickly to destabilizing movements from three different positions.

Setup

Sitting on a flat bench, place a ball beside you and extend your arm out to the side so your hand sits on top of the ball. You should be pressing down quite firmly on the ball, not allowing any movement. Maintain a tall posture with the chest up, and set your abdominals.

Movement

While you are pressing down on the ball, your partner begins slapping the ball in multiple directions with about 60 to 75 percent force. Use maximal effort to prevent any kind of movement in the ball. Although the photo demonstrates the arm in a position of lateral abduction, this exercise can be performed with the arm in multiple positions (such as extended in front or at a 45-degree angle).

Finish

The set is completed when the number of ball slaps is completed (20 to 30 rapid ball slaps are recommended).

Most shoulder problems are a result of weak musculature on the posterior side of the shoulder and in the muscles that span from the spine over the scapula. This exercise strengthens those muscles and provides balance between the stronger muscles in the front of the shoulder to those in the back.

Setup

Use a ball that allows your arms to be in the fully extended position toward the floor while you are holding dumbbells. With dumbbells in hand, lie over the ball so the ball is under your sternum. Your shoulders, hips, and knees fall in line.

Movement

Contract the muscles of your lower trapezius so that your scapulae slide downward toward your rib cage. This movement can be described as depressing your shoulders. As you reach the end range for your scapulae, begin to externally rotate your hands to further work these muscles.

a

Finish

Once you have fully externally rotated your shoulders, hold this position for two to three seconds and return to the start position.

b

MEDICINE BALL SHOULDER-TO-SHOULDER PASS

 This drill develops strength in the shoulder and back region and links the strength through the legs, hips, torso, and upper body. In its advanced forms, balance, proprioception, and countermovement mechanics are all emphasized.

Setup

Stand facing your partner, about three paces apart. Keep your feet shoulder-width apart, knees slightly flexed, and abdominals precontracted.

Movement

Partner A positions a hand and the medicine ball directly in front of the right shoulder. The pass line goes from the right shoulder to partner B's right shoulder. Partner B prepares to receive the ball by flexing the knees, contracting the core, and fully extending the arms, giving the partner a target. The goal is to "cushion" the pass reception with the entire body. The ball comes into the hands and the arms bend, drawing in the ball closer to the right shoulder. The hips drop and the body weight shifts onto the right leg, flexing at the knee. This is a whole-body catch. The pass back reverses the flow. The pass begins by pushing the foot into the floor, extending the leg, rotating with the hip and torso, and finally extending the arms to thrust the ball back to partner A. The arm movement is more of a direct push from the shoulder (similar to a shot put) rather than a throw in baseball.

Finish

Continue this sequence for a set number of repetitions. Repeat the set from left shoulder to left shoulder.

Tips and Progressions

- One-arm shoulder-to-shoulder pass: Execute the same technique and progression with one arm only. To catch the ball, you will rely more on absorbing and cushioning the ball with your entire body. It becomes a torso and lower-body catch. You will also rely on the quality of the pass. When first attempting this advanced exercise, your partner will tend to lob a soft and arced pass, which is difficult to catch. A crisp, straight pass from shoulder to shoulder will be easier to cushion and balance.

- One-arm and opposite-leg shoulder-to-shoulder pass: Follow the same exercise instruction but balance on one leg only. For the pass from right shoulder to right shoulder, both partners balance on the left leg. Superior balance, proprioception, core and hip stabilization, and multijoint pass reception are all challenged.

a

b

MEDICINE BALL SOCCER THROW-IN PASSES

This soccer-specific exercise develops great lat strength and back power. It expands the torso and requires solid core stability.

Setup

Both partners stand facing each other, about two paces apart. Keep your feet shoulder-width apart, knees slightly flexed, and abdominals precontracted. Partner A sets up by holding the ball above the head.

Movement

Partner A begins by lowering the ball behind the head, then pulls the ball back overhead, releasing the ball once the arms are fully extended and hands are about one foot (30 centimeters) forward of the body. The pass is aimed above partner B's head.

Finish

Partner B catches the ball high above the head, about one inch (2.5 centimeters) in front of the head. The pass is cushioned by absorbing the ball and slowing down its momentum progressively until the ball is behind the head. Additional knee flexion during pass reception will absorb the pass and protect the lower back. Return the pass and continue for the desired number of reps.

Tips and Progressions

- Catch low passes by dropping quickly into a squat position, dropping the hips, and flexing the knees as much as needed to catch the ball overhead.
- We also prescribe this as an advanced progression. The pass can be thrown low, so you squat and catch, and drive up with knee extension on the return pass.

a

b

This exercise focuses on the posterior chain to strengthen the back and posterior delts.

Setup

Stand facing away from a wall, feet shoulder-width apart, knees flexed, core set and braced, middle back set, and shoulders and elbows flexed to 90 degrees. Rotate at the shoulder so your elbow is level with the shoulder, and press a DSL stability ball into the wall. A stronger push is needed against a DSL ball to overcome the load (weight of the ball). Hold for five seconds.

Movement

Moving the arms, torso, and feet, rotate around toward the ball so you end up facing the ball with both forearms pressing against the ball.

Finish

Remove the original arm and rotate out away from the ball. Finish by facing away from the ball, the new arm and shoulder engaged to hold the ball in place. Hold this arm for five seconds before alternating sides.

Tips and Progressions

At the five-second hold position, maintain neutral posture, avoiding a lumbar arch to compensate for lack of shoulder girdle strength. When strength progresses, graduate to a full shoulder extension. When in the ball hold position, facing away from the wall, extend the arm up overhead and hold that finish position for five seconds (see photo *b*). This will require strength to push the ball *up* the wall, as well as strength to press the ball *into* the wall to resist gravity that is acting on the DSL load.

a

b

Abdominals, Lower Back, and Glutes

Exercises in This Chapter

This exercise is borrowed from traditional floor-based sit-ups. Refined technique is required so that you can feel the same burn in the abs that you would with floor-based crunches and sit-ups. Ball wrap sit-ups deliver superior strength results because the shape of the ball allows safe torso wrapping to prestretch the abdominals, allowing them to work through a greater range of motion. The shape of the ball is more comfortable on the back and better targets abdominals instead of firing hip flexors.

Setup

The setup position is key to the concentric contraction achieved at the peak of the sit-up. Sit on top of the ball and roll forward slightly. Feet are on the floor, shoulder-width apart. The setup is actually positioned at the midpoint of the exercise because its accuracy determines the level of abdominal overload achieved. When you sit up on the ball, you should hold a contraction and have the low back off the ball.

Movement

After setting the core, slowly lower, under control, onto the ball and continue to wrap right over the ball. Lower under control to work the eccentric muscle contraction. Avoid clasping hands behind the head. Instead, just make sure the arms are "quiet," whether they are crossed on your chest or flexed at your side. Keep them stationary through the movement to remove any momentum.

Middle Position

At the midpoint, pause at the end of the eccentric loading and sense the stretch before initiating movement back up and off the ball. Although you are actually only slightly wrapped around the ball, your perception is that you are almost upside down.

Finish

Slowly lift your trunk up off of the ball, segment by segment, until you are sitting upright, resting on your glutes.

Tips and Progressions

- Adopting a wider base of support can make this exercise easier.
- Advance the level of difficulty by placing your feet together, which requires greater muscle activation to stabilize on the ball during movement than does the wider base of support.
- After successful training with a narrow base, close your eyes to increase the demands. Any time you sense a loss of balance, open your eyes.

a

b

ADAM'S MEDICINE BALL AB LOCKOUT

 This is an excellent move that requires a partner. The exercise fires your rectus abdominis muscle. It was developed by Adam Douglas, a strength coach at the Athletic Conditioning Center. The key is not only the abdominal work but also the tie-in of the adductors to hold on to the medicine ball. This is an excellent method of integrating muscles in both the frontal plane and sagittal plane.

Setup

Lie on your back with your legs up in a 90-degree angle and your fingers touching your temples. Squeeze a medicine ball between your knees. Your elbows should be in contact with your thighs.

Movement

Once you are in this position, hold your elbows tight to your thighs. A partner grabs onto your knees and pulls you forward.

Finish

As you are pulled forward, stay very tight. Do not let your elbows come off your thighs.

Tips and Progressions

To increase the difficulty of this exercise, your partner can use a faster and slower speed of rocking your body. The pull should never be explosive, just a controlled motion.

ABDOMINAL SIDE CRUNCH

This exercise focuses on the muscles that allow you to bend side to side: the obliques and quadratus lumborum. These muscles are important for flexibility and stability of your core.

Setup

Place a ball approximately three to four feet (about a meter) from a wall. Sit on the ball so that your hips are at the apex of the ball and your feet are against the wall. Stabilize your feet against the wall so you do not roll forward. Lie across the ball so you bend laterally over it.

Movement

From the supported position, begin by crunching laterally until your knees, hips, and shoulders are all in line.

Finish

Once you have reached the position where your body is in line, return to the starting position, ensuring that you fully extend back over the ball.

Tips and Progressions

- As in the abdominal crunch, there are many variations for the side crunch. You can progress from holding your arms across your chest to holding your hands by your ears and then extending your arms over your head.
- You can add an external load by holding a dumbbell in front of your chest.
- By using a medicine ball, you can add a ballistic component to the drill by performing a side crunch throw to a partner.

This is an effective method of adding resistance to the lower-abdominal muscles. This area is key in controlling pelvic positioning, which can play a factor in decreasing low back pain.

Setup

Lying on the floor, with your legs over the ball, place a cable with an ankle strap around your ankles. Your hands should be under your lower back, at the navel level. Make sure that your back maintains contact with your hands. This ensures proper low back posture during the exercise.

Movement

Set your core and bring your knees toward your chest. Focus on not allowing your back to arch off the floor as you bring your knees up and back.

Finish

Once you have reached a point where your legs are just past the 90-degree point, slowly return to the start position.

Safety Point

If you cannot maintain your posture with the added load of the cable, then you should focus on performing the movement without the cable, progress to a medicine ball between your legs, and then try the cable again.

a

b

SUPINE LOWER-ABDOMINAL CURL AND CRUNCH

 This is the most advanced lower-abdominal exercise you will perform. It focuses on pelvic strength, stability, and balance.

Setup

Set a ball in front of something solid you can hold on to. The side of a power rack or a loaded barbell will do. Lie over the ball so that your lower back is supported by the curve of the ball and your knees are bent. Hold on to a rack overhead to stabilize yourself.

Movement

Begin by setting your core, and focus on uncurling your pelvis off of the curve of the ball. You will accomplish this by slowly bringing your knees toward you. As your legs reach the 90-degree point, try to touch the ceiling with your knees by lifting your pelvis higher in a reverse crunch position.

Finish

Once you have reached up as high as you can, hold that position for two to three seconds, then slowly return to the start position by reversing your movements.

a

b

V-SIT MEDICINE BALL TRANSFER

This exercise challenges the core through a range of motion from extension to core flexion.

Setup

Lie on your back with arms fully extended over your head holding a medicine ball.

Movement

Begin by engaging your core and flexing at the waist. This will cause your legs and arms to rise at the same time. Flex forward until you can transfer the medicine ball from your hands to your feet.

Finish

Once you have transferred the ball to your feet, lower back to the starting position and repeat.

Tips and Progressions

- Ensure that as you flex forward your arms remain extended overhead.
- This exercise is quite advanced and challenging. You might want to begin with transferring a stability ball before progressing to a medicine ball.

a

b

This exercise focuses on the lower abdominals and forces them to overcome resistance. The load and time under tension quickly fatigue the musculature and produce great strength gains.

Setup

Begin by lying faceup on the floor. Your hands are on the floor just underneath your glutes. Place one foot at each side of the ball and press inward. A coach or partner gets into position beside the ball.

Movement

Lift the ball up off the floor, flex at the knees, and pull the ball up and over the chest, allowing the hips to come up off the floor. Think of producing an arc from the floor to the middle position up over the chest. The partner applies resistance to the ball with the hands, resisting your direction of travel. Surprisingly, a very light resistance will be a challenge.

Finish

Once the ball is up over the chest, the partner is finished applying resistance. Slowly lower the ball back to the floor under control. Maintain a pelvic tilt to prevent excessive arching through the lumbar spine.

Tips and Progressions

Communicate with your partner to determine the optimal amount of resistance.

a

b

REVERSE BACK EXTENSION

 This great exercise works the lower back. It uses both a ball and a bench, and the difficulty can be increased by using a cable attached to the ankles.

Setup

Place a stability ball on top of a flat bench, and lie over the ball while grasping the sides of the bench for support.

Movement

Begin by setting your core before attempting to extend the hips and legs. Your head and neck should also maintain a neutral position. Just before you begin to extend your hips and legs, activate the glutes by squeezing them to ensure that they initiate the movement.

Finish

The legs should be raised to a point where the knees, hips, and shoulders are all in line. Hold the contracted position for a second, and lower to the original position.

Tips and Progressions

You can slowly work up to the reverse hyperextension as the end of a long, safe progression. The following are some examples:

1. Begin with the ball on the floor and hands braced on the floor for balance. Extend the hips. Begin with an underinflated ball, and progress to full inflation.

2. Place the ball on a bench and perform movement with no external resistance. Begin with an underinflated ball, and progress to full inflation.

3. Hold a 5- to 10-pound dumbbell (or a 2.5- to 5-kilogram dumbbell) between the ankles, and extend the hips.

4. Progress to full reverse hyperextension with cable.

a

b

The back extension is an important movement in integrating the low back, glutes, and hamstrings. This exercise has been traditionally performed on a back extension bench. The stability ball allows for training in balance.

Setup

Place a stability ball in front of you, and lie over it. Your center of gravity should be just slightly behind the center of the ball. When starting out, ensure that your legs are wide enough apart to provide a good base of support to initiate the movement.

Movement

Place your hands by your ears, set your abdominals, activate your glutes, and slowly rise to the point at which your shoulders, hips, and knees are in a fairly straight line. Hold this position.

Finish

Slowly lower yourself back to the initial position, providing a stretch to your low back.

Tips and Progressions

- Bring legs closer together, decreasing your base of support and increasing the stability factor.
- Hold arms out straight with thumbs pointing to the ceiling (as in a superman pose) to increase the lever arm length and stress to the back and glutes.

This exercise provides a low-load method to preferentially contract the lats while integrating low back and glutes along the posterior chain.

Setup

Kneel behind a DSL stability ball. Roll on top and over the ball into a plank push-up position, hips over the ball so the torso is off the front and legs are off the back of the ball. Contract the glutes to keep the legs out straight, and contract the core to stay on top of the ball.

Movement

Keeping the hands in place, push back until arms are stretched out in front of the shoulders. With the arms straight, pull the body back across the ball into a push-up position.

Tips and Progressions

- To regress this exercise, set up with hands closer to the ball and more of your body on the opposite side to the point where the toes are on the floor.
- You can get more of a challenge by setting up with the hands farther away from the ball.

a

b

BALL SIT-UP TO MEDICINE BALL PASS

The medicine ball pass adds a dynamic load to a foundational abdominal exercise. Catching a medicine ball imposes distally loaded torque, which must be absorbed and decelerated under control. An additional challenge is the instability at the top of the stability ball where body weight loads and on the floor at the bottom of the stability ball.

Setup

Partner A is positioned on the stability ball, sitting about one-third of the way down the front side of the ball with feet flat on the floor and hip-width apart. With little or no movement of the stability ball, partner A rolls back on the ball, allowing the back to conform around the ball. Partner A has the medicine ball in the hands, ready to do a chest pass to partner B at the end of the sit-up. Partner B stands about four feet (approximately a meter) away from partner A in a good athletic stance, ready to give and receive the medicine ball passes.

Movement

From the start position, partner A engages the abdominal wall and sits up—not curls up—keeping the neck in a neutral position. As partner A approaches the top phase of the sit-up, partner A chest passes the ball to partner B, releasing the ball from the fingertips.

Middle Position

At the top phase, partner A should have the abdominal wall engaged in a neutral alignment from the hips to the neck. The hip joint is angled slightly greater than 90 degrees. In this position the low back is off the ball, and the glutes are on the top, front side of the ball. In the middle position, the core remains contracted. If partner A continues forward to a point at which the core relaxes, lean back slightly until the core engages again. In this position, partner A has the hands out in front, creating the target for partner B to pass the ball back.

Finish

Partner B chest passes the ball back to partner A who absorbs the pass by immediately engaging the core muscles and rolls back down to the start position.

Tips and Progressions

- Start off with slow, controlled sit-ups and partner passes from chest to chest.
- To advance, increase the weight of the medicine ball, increase the rep count, or increase the tempo of both the throw velocity and sit-up speed.
- Another challenge can be added by increasing the length of partner A's levers by extending the arms overhead during the throw and catch. In this variation, in the down phase of the sit-up, the ball is held overhead instead of in front of the chest.

Biceps,
Triceps,
and Forearms

9

Exercises in This Chapter

The purpose of the technique in this variation of the biceps curl is to provide a means of sensing proper posture and also to provide a means of focusing solely on the biceps movement.

Setup

A partner works with you to place the ball between you and the wall. Ball placement should be at shoulder blade level. As you stand against the ball, your chest should be up and you should stand tall but with a slight bend in your knees. You should feel the ball with the backs of your arms (triceps) at all times. This ensures that you maintain a straight arm position, which will enhance biceps recruitment.

Movement

Keeping your eyes focused straight ahead, begin by pulling in your navel and then flexing at your elbows. Curl the dumbbells to the point where you can flex your arm no farther.

Finish

Once you have reached the fully flexed position, begin a slow descent back to the starting position. Lower the weight all the way down to the point at which your elbows are fully extended.

a   b

ECCENTRIC ACCENTUATED BICEPS CURL

 An eccentric contraction occurs when a muscle lengthens under load. Eccentric contractions are known to be significantly stronger than concentric contractions (in which a muscle shortens under load). In the biceps curl movement, as you lower the weight, you can actually lower a heavier weight than what you could raise. If you work on emphasizing the eccentric portion of the movement, your potential concentric (lifting) strength will increase.

Setup

Use a ball that will allow you to lie over it prone with your arms fully extended. Select a weight that is 20 to 40 percent heavier than what you would normally use.

Movement

Since the weight is significantly heavier than what you would normally use, to raise the weight you will need to roll back on the ball. This rolling back will provide you with a mechanical advantage, assisting you in raising the weight.

Finish

Once you have the weight in a fully flexed position, roll back so that your upper arm is back in the downward extended position. Begin by extending your elbow very slowly. It should take you four to six seconds to lower the weight. Once your arm is fully extended, reposition yourself for the next repetition.

a

b

OVERHEAD MEDICINE BALL WALL BOUNCE

This drill challenges speed and hand reaction. The movement itself is specific to a throw-in in soccer and overhead pass in basketball. In sports, speed and explosive movement are critical factors, and this movement allows you to move fast.

Setup

Stand approximately three to four feet (about a meter) away from a wall, with your body in a good athletic position with your core engaged. Hold the medicine ball overhead and flex your elbows so that the ball is actually held behind your head. Elbows should point directly toward the ceiling.

Movement

While you maintain your elbow position, rapidly extend your elbows so that you release the ball toward the wall. Maintain your core position while extending the elbows.

Finish

The ball will come off the wall very quickly. Make sure your hands are ready to accept the ball. The momentum of the ball off the wall will provide a ballistic stretch to your triceps. This elastic loading is then used in reloading and following through on your next rep.

Tips and Progressions

Think of the ball as a hot lava rock. You do not want to hold on to a ball that is hot for very long. The less time you spend with the ball in your hands, the more you will develop the elastic properties of the triceps muscle.

a

b

INCLINE TRICEPS EXTENSION

The incline triceps extension provides a great challenge to the triceps muscle, specifically the long head of the triceps. As a result of the overhead position of the arms, the long head will get a little more work than the other parts of the triceps.

Setup

Lie over the stability ball on your back. Once in this position, roll forward to a position in which the ball supports your head, shoulders, and back. Once in this position, raise your arms overhead in an extended position with dumbbells in hand.

Movement

While maintaining an erect upper arm, bend at the elbow joint, lowering the dumbbells to a point where you reach full elbow flexion. The dumbbells should be on each side of your head at this point.

Finish

To finish this movement, return to the starting position. Keep your elbows pointing straight up, which will provide optimal isolation for your triceps.

a

b

This is an advanced exercise that you should attempt only if you are very experienced. Attempt this first with the feet on the floor; as you become stronger you can perform it with the feet raised on a bench.

Setup

Place both hands on the ball and the feet on the floor with your back in a tight supported position with your abdominals drawn in.

Movement

Holding your back and posture in a very tight position, begin the movement by dropping your elbows toward the floor. The movement can be described as wrapping your forearms down and around the ball.

Finish

As you reach the bottom position after dropping your elbows, your body will be challenged to stay on the ball. Maintain your position and extend your arms to bring yourself back to the starting position.

a

b

This exercise uses the simplicity of push-ups and adds balance, core stability, and increased strength requirements.

Setup

Place a medicine ball in front of you. Get into prone position with the hands on the ball in push-up position. Set abdominals to maintain a strong trunk (straight line from ankles to shoulders). Hands are at 3 o'clock and 9 o'clock on the ball. For a greater challenge place feet together to create a small platform, increasing the balance requirements.

Movement

Keeping a rigid core, flex the elbows and lower under control, moving the chest toward the top of the ball.

Finish

Hold and balance before extending the arms to push the body back up in a push-up position.

a

b

WRIST CURL AND EXTENSION

The setup is the same for both wrist curls and wrist extensions. Flexion and extension of the wrist are areas that traditionally have been ignored in strengthening programs, mainly because people think that these muscles receive enough work during other gripping exercises.

Setup

Set up in front of an adjustable cable column, or hold dumbbells, as shown in the photos. Set the column so that the pulley is approximately 20 degrees below the top of the ball.

Movement

Grasping the bar with an underhand grip for the curl movement, begin in the fully extended position and flex your wrists through a full range of motion. Hold this position for a second or two.

Finish

Slowly lower the weight back to the original position.

Note: For the extension movement, palms begin facing the floor.

a

b

MEDICINE BALL WALK-OVER

 Walk-overs are similar to push-ups but activate many more muscles to handle the uneven surfaces and single-arm loading.

Setup

Place a ball in front of you. Get into prone position with the hands on the ball in push-up position. Set the abdominals to maintain a strong trunk (straight line from ankles to shoulders). Remove your left hand and set it on the floor to the left of the ball. Feet remain in place, but upper-body load shifts over to the left arm (floor hand) as you lower onto the left arm.

Movement

Extend the left arm, then push up and over the ball. Transfer your weight onto the right hand as the left hand leaves the floor and joins the right hand on the ball. Once stable, shift your weight onto the left hand and pick up the right hand, placing it on the floor off to the right of the ball.

Finish

Shift your weight over to the right arm. Lower into a push-up position. Continue this sequence until fatigue prevents safe execution.

Tips and Progressions

Power-over: Using the same general technique and progression, power-overs add a plyometric action. When extending the floor (left) arm, powerfully drive up to propel the torso into the air. The right hand leaves the ball slightly before the left hand lands on the ball. The torso shifts left and right with speed. When the right hand reaches the floor, quickly flex the elbow to drop into a push-up position and immediately explode back up, pushing the torso back up and over the ball. The hands dance back and forth, executing this drill with speed.

a

b

MEDICINE BALL QUICK DROP AND CATCH

Grip strength and forearm development are important for sports that require grip on an implement or object. Holding on to a hockey stick or tennis racket and a pump fake in football are examples of the need for grip strength with integrated forearm movement.

Setup

Begin in an athletic position facing your partner, who is holding a smaller-diameter medicine ball. Place your hands in a pronated, or palms-down, position. Your elbows should be in close to your body at 90-degree angles.

Movement

The exercise begins when your partner releases the ball. After the release, very quickly extend your elbows eccentrically in the direction of the dropping ball.

Finish

Catch the ball within 4 to 6 inches (10 to 15 centimeters) of its drop, and flex the elbows back up so that you have 90-degree angles at the elbows.

Tips and Progressions

This movement should be completed very fast. Think of the ball as being very hot. If you hold on too long, you will burn your hand.

a

b

Whole Body

Exercises in This Chapter

This exercise combines a standing rollout with a leg press. It builds leg strength and hip stability during the leg press along with trunk and shoulder strength in the standing position.

Setup

Partner A lies supine on the floor with knees flexed, feet in the air, and core set. Partner B stands up in front of partner A's feet to hold a stability ball between partner A's feet and partner B's hands. Partner B has flexed knees, body weight loaded on the legs, and arms flexed.

Movement

As partner A moves the legs to bring the ball toward the hips, partner B shifts weight onto the hands and over the ball, elevating the heels to pivot forward on the toes.

Finish

With partner B's weight over the ball, partner A extends the legs to push the ball away from the body. Partner B must work to keep stabilized on the ball, because it might travel slightly outside the midline during the exercise.

Tips and Progressions

There is a tendency to focus on the leg press action. Also pay attention to the standing rollout, which is a more complex maneuver to master. Once partners get over the learning curve, they will benefit greatly from this exercise.

a

b

SQUAT TO OVERHEAD PRESS

This is a great whole-body, multijoint exercise done in a simple movement pattern.

Setup

Begin in a standing position with feet shoulder-width apart, core set and braced, and middle back set. Hold a DSL stability ball at shoulder height with hands pressing inward. Double-check scapular retraction.

Movement

Maintaining solid posture, squat by lowering the glutes and hips back into a seated position. At midpoint knees are above the toes (not out past the toes and not dropping inward). As you extend the legs to stand up, also extend the arms to press the ball overhead.

Finish

Maintain a standing position and lower the weighted ball under control to shoulder height before lowering into the next squat. Do not fall into a protracted shoulder position.

Tips and Progressions

- Check for a smooth whole-body sequence and clean line of travel by listening to the dynamic stabilizing load—it should *not* shift inside the ball and should not make a sound.
- Once your shoulders fatigue, finish each rep by lowering the ball to shoulder height *at the same time* that you lower back into a squat.

a

b

David Weck is the creator of the BOSU device and most recently the DSL stability ball. David has created some outstanding exercises with the BOSU and the DSL ball. This is just one of his exercises that combines functional agility with a fun movement. The ball allows you to complete rolling movements safely without the impact usually associated with this type of athletic drill.

Setup

Get in position beside the ball in a deep split stance position with the outside leg forward and inside hand on the floor.

Movement

Drop the torso onto the ball and roll right over, exiting off the opposite side.

Finish

Land in a deep split stance with the outside leg forward and inside hand on the floor to help steady the body. Finish with your head up, visually aware, before returning across the ball to the first side.

Tips and Progressions

- Begin slowly, striving for control and consistency.
- When you become proficient, start to increase the tempo.

a

b

WALKING LUNGE WITH OVERHEAD MEDICINE BALL ROTATION

The walking lunge on its own is quite a challenging exercise. When you add the extra load of the medicine ball with overhead rotation, you create a movement that encompasses flexion, extension, and rotation. Although the prime mover is the legs, this movement challenges the whole body.

Setup

Begin in a split position so that the front of the tibia is perpendicular to the floor with a 90-degree angle at the knee. If you begin with your left leg in front, you will hold the ball with the core rotated to the left and the ball on the outside of the left hip.

Movement

To initiate movement, press the left foot into the floor, which will initiate extension of the left hip and left quad. As this firing of the quad and hip begins, raise the ball up in a half-circle motion overhead. The right leg also begins to step forward with the goal of becoming the forward plant leg.

Middle Position

In the middle position you should have the ball right overhead, and your left leg should be fully extended.

Finish

As the right foot comes forward and lowers into a flexed position at the knee, the ball continues to move overhead in the half-circle motion to finish on the opposite hip.

Tips and Progressions

You can also use this walking lunge movement with a static overhead medicine ball hold. This provides greater challenge to the posterior chain musculature, which will promote proper posture.

a

b

ANGLE LUNGE WITH HORIZONTAL MEDICINE BALL ROTATION

 This exercise is similar to the walking lunge. The difference is that this is performed while in place, with a greater challenge to the medial adductors of the thigh.

Setup

Begin in a split position so that the front of the tibia is perpendicular to the floor with a 90-degree angle at the knee and the hip abducted to approximately 30 to 40 degrees. If you begin with your left leg in front, the ball will be held with the core rotated to the left and arms extended straight out at chest height.

Movement

To initiate movement, press the left foot into the floor, which will initiate extension of the left hip and left quad. As this firing of the quad and hip begins, rotate the medicine ball across your body, horizontal to the floor.

Middle Position

In the middle position you should have the ball right in front of your chest and your left leg coming back to the midline of the body. Here there is an instantaneous transfer of weight, and the right leg begins to explode to a 30- to 40-degree angle to the right side.

Finish

As the right foot comes forward and lowers into a flexed position at the knee, the ball continues to move across the body to finish on the right side.

Tips and Progressions

If you have difficulty keeping your posture correct as you rotate and move, try shortening the lever by holding the ball closer to the body, and progress to fully extended arms.

a

b

MEDICINE BALL WALKING PUSH-UP

This exercise is an advanced version of the medicine ball push-up. There is more coordination of the total body as you maneuver yourself over five medicine balls.

Setup

Place five balls in a row approximately 2 to 3 feet apart (about 61 to 91 centimeters). Begin by placing one hand on top of a medicine ball and the opposite hand on the floor. Your body should be engaged as you maintain good posture for this push-up position.

Movement

Beginning in the down position, press yourself up and over each ball. The hand movement during the transfer is very quick, so make sure that you have solid hand placement on the ball before you descend.

Finish

Work your way to the end of the line, and then progress back to your first ball.

Tips and Progressions

- If you cannot make it back to the first ball, start with only three or four balls and progress to five.
- You can also complete movement in only one direction as your first set. Then rest and return in the opposite direction.
- For an added challenge, try using balls of different sizes.

a

b

MEDICINE BALL LATERAL TO FRONT OVERHEAD THROW TO WALL

This combines movement from the frontal to sagittal planes via movement through the transverse plane. From a sport perspective, there is also an explosive overhead movement ending with a powerful eccentric contraction on the lead leg. This multidirectional movement is what functional training is all about.

Setup

Begin by standing with one shoulder facing the wall. Hips and knees should be slightly flexed in a good athletic position. Hold the medicine ball at approximately hip height. You are now ready to initiate the movement.

Movement

The initiation of movement comes from your hips, where there is a weight shift from the leg closest to the wall to the leg farthest from the wall. At the same time the ball begins to swing back into a loaded position overhead.

Finish

Once the ball is overhead, begin to rotate your shoulders so that they are facing the wall. As you begin the rotation, you will also drive off of the back leg to assist in the rocket throw against the wall. The front leg is off the floor as you lunge forward to throw, decelerating your body with the front leg.

Tips and Progressions

- The weight shift is the key to success in this drill. The transfer must come from the floor up to optimize the power to the ball.
- Start with a lighter ball to ensure proper technique.
- You can also try this as a chest press movement to emphasize pushing over throwing.

a

b

This minicircuit is a combination of four movements in one giant set. It will tax your core as well as your anaerobic energy system.

Overhead Chop

Set up in a solid athletic stance, feet shoulder-width apart, with your chest and shoulders just over your knees. Hold a medicine ball with your arms fully extended so that the ball is between your knees. Set your core before initiating the following movement.

Swing your arms straight up hard so the ball will move up overhead, just as you might swing an ax (see photo *a*).

Once you have reached the overhead position, reverse your movement as fast as you can, and drive the ball back down with a powerful chop. Reverse the movement again and continue until you complete 10 chops.

Once you have completed the 10 overhead chops, the second consecutive movement is the overhead lateral side bend.

Overhead Lateral Side Bend

Maintaining the same athletic stance, hold the ball overhead in a fully extended arm position.

Set your core and laterally flex at your waist so you bend over to one side (see photo *b*). Do not allow any lateral movement as you flex sideways.

Once you have flexed laterally as far as you can, reverse the direction to the opposite side. The movement speed should not be explosive, but it should be fast. Complete 10 flexions to each side, then move on to the standing twist.

Standing Twist

Continue the same solid athletic stance, and flex your arms forward so the ball is held out front at chest level.

Using an explosive movement, rotate to one side. Ensure that you follow the ball with your eyes and head as you turn (see photo *c*).

Once you have reached your full range of rotation, explosively rotate back to the opposite side, again following the ball with your eyes and head. Complete 10 rotations to each side.

The final exercise is the ax chop with hip flexion, which ties in the upper and lower body in a complex movement.

Ax Chop With Hip Flexion

Immediately after your last standing rotation, move the ball up over one shoulder, and slide the opposite leg back on an angle of approximately 30 degrees.

Begin the movement by simultaneously chopping down with the ball and flexing your opposite hip up with a very fast movement (see photo *d*).

Once the ball has met the outside of the thigh, return to the original start position. Complete 10 repetitions to each side and then rest.

Once you have completed one full minicircuit, rest 60 to 120 seconds and repeat three or four circuits.

a

b

c

d

AX CHOP WITH HIP FLEXION

This movement ties in the functional line of the right external oblique, left hip adductor, psoas, and rectus femoris. This line of pull can be traced from the top of the right ilium to the middle outer thigh. These muscles all function together to provide rotation to the left. The movement should begin with a moderate pace.

Setup

Get in a solid athletic stance with your feet approximately shoulder-width apart. Holding the ball with both hands, flex your arms up so that the ball is up over the shoulder. Slide your opposite leg back on an angle of approximately 30 degrees.

Movement

Begin the movement by simultaneously chopping down with the ball and flexing your opposite hip up with a slight adduction. This will produce a crisscross of the ball and your upper thigh.

Finish

Once the ball has met the outside of the thigh, reverse the movement quickly and return to the start position.

Tips and Progressions

- Once you feel comfortable with a moderate speed, progress to a more explosive movement.
- You can provide added resistance to the hip flexors and adductors by attaching rubber tubing or a cable to your ankle.

a

b

This drill requires some coordination in driving the ball into the floor at the correct angle to catch and reverse the movement.

Setup

With feet shoulder-width apart, raise the ball overhead and over to one side. Set your core and prepare to drive the ball downward.

Movement

Success in this drill is determined by the angle needed to receive the ball. As you drive the ball down from your outside shoulder, you want to hit a midpoint on the floor between your feet. This will cause the ball to bounce up on an angle toward the opposite shoulder.

Finish

Once you have released the ball, your arms move to the opposite side to meet the ball and begin deceleration. The bounce of the ball should take your hands up to the opposite shoulder. Then explode the ball back in the opposite direction.

Tips and Progressions

Begin this movement with a lighter ball in the 6- to 8-pound range (about 2.5 to 3.5 kilograms), and slowly progress until you can handle a 12- to 15-pound (about 5.5 to 6.5 kilograms) medicine ball.

a

b

MEDICINE BALL OVERHEAD JUMP AND THROW

This exercise may very well be the most integrated explosive medicine ball exercise you can perform. It requires an explosive triple extension of the body (integration of the ankles, knees, and hips). This movement is important if you play football, compete in track and field events, or would just like to work on your total-body explosiveness.

Setup

With feet shoulder-width apart and your body in a set athletic position, hold the medicine ball so it hangs right below your shoulders at approximately knee level.

Movement

Begin the movement by driving your hips forward and pressing your feet into the floor. This will be a powerful and fast muscle contraction. This initial drive results in a force in which your body propels itself upward in a jumping motion.

Finish

As your body drives upward, integrate the upward movement of the ball. Use the momentum of your jump and transfer that force to the ball. Release the ball as your arms rise to the highest point of your jump.

Tips and Progressions

- Begin this movement with a lighter ball in the 12- to 15-pound range (about 5.5 to 6.5 kilograms), and slowly progress until you can handle a 25- to 30-pound (about 11 to 13.5 kilograms) medicine ball. This heavier weight will challenge your nervous system.

- You can drive the ball either straight up into the air or in a backward arc. When the ball goes straight up, make sure you do not try to catch it. Get out of the way and let it fall to the floor. When throwing back in an arc, you should be outdoors and ensure no one is in the ball's path.

a

b

MEDICINE BALL THROW TWO-LEG JUMP TO SINGLE-LEG LATERAL LAND

 This drill is excellent for coordination and power combined. It involves power in both the sagittal and frontal planes and deceleration, which are important for sports that require changes in direction.

Setup

You should be approximately 8 to 10 feet (2.4 to 3 meters) from a solid wall or a partner that you can throw the ball into. Be set in an athletic stance while holding the ball close to the chest at chest height.

Movement

This movement is quite complex and you may want to refer to the DVD for a more appropriate representation of the technique. The initial movement involves simultaneously driving the ball into the wall and jumping forward.

Finish

As you propel yourself forward, you must turn 90 degrees and land on your inside leg closest to the wall. Stabilize when you land, and catch the ball as it comes off the wall. Once you catch the ball, reset your position and repeat.

Tips and Progressions

You can try progressing your single-leg landing to the outside leg, which will stress the landing adductors. Before attempting with the ball, try a few repetitions without the ball and make sure you are familiar with the footwork.

Flexibility

Exercises in This Chapter

Mobility in the spine is essential if the rest of the body is to function efficiently. As with strengthening, stretching the spine in multiple planes and angles will assist in spinal health. The spinal extension is a safe method of placing a stretch on the anterior ligaments and muscles of the spinal column as well as the abdominals.

Setup

Sitting on a ball, walk forward until the ball lies in the natural curve of your lower back.

Movement

Rock forward and backward by pressing your legs into the floor. This will force the ball to roll back. Follow the roll of the ball, which will provide the stretch to the abdominals. The farther you roll back, the greater the stretch. Begin with smaller rolls at first and then progress to larger rolls.

Finish

Once you have reached your end range, hold the stretch for 8 to 15 seconds, and then return. This stretch time is shorter than for most stretches because with your head in this position, you may feel slightly dizzy if you stay in the stretched position for an extended period.

This drill provides a stretch for the all important side-flexing spinal muscles as well as the obliques.

Setup

Place a ball approximately three to four feet (about a meter) from a wall. Sit on the ball so that your hips are at the apex of the ball and your feet are against the wall. Stabilize your feet against the wall so you do not roll forward. Lie across the ball so you bend laterally over it.

Movement

There is no movement once you have reached the stretched position.

Finish

Hold the stretched position over the ball for 20 to 30 seconds, then repeat on the opposite side.

The hamstrings, which are on the backs of the thighs, are typically some of the tightest muscles in the body and can limit flexibility around the hip and lower back. The supine hamstring stretch provides a static and dynamic challenge for the hamstring muscle group at both the hip and knee joint.

Setup

Place a ball between a wall and your feet, and walk the ball up the wall so that your legs are extended. If your hamstrings are very inflexible, you will need to position yourself farther back from the wall.

Movement

Keeping your pelvis in contact with the floor, begin to roll the ball up the wall by extending your legs. Once your legs are fully extended, hold this position for 20 to 30 seconds and return to the start position. You can also perform dynamic stretches by moving the ball faster in an up-and-down motion. Perform 15 to 20 movements before resting.

Tips and Progressions

- As you become more flexible, slide your body closer to the wall before the leg movement.
- Move progressively in small increments to prevent your pelvis from coming off the floor as you move closer.

a   b

STANDING HAMSTRING STRETCH

Stretching the hamstring from the standing position will emphasize the upper part of the muscle toward the hip.

Setup

Place your foot on top of a ball.

Movement

Maintain your lordotic curve in the lower back, and slowly flex forward. Focus on moving your navel toward your thigh. At the same time as you flex forward, press your heel gently into the ball. Hold this contraction for five to six seconds, relax the stretch for two seconds, and then proceed into the next stretch. This uses the proprioceptive neuromuscular facilitation (PNF) method of stretching, which means that if you contract a muscle, allow it to relax, and then stretch it again, the subsequent stretch will be greater. You can also focus on the different heads of the hamstrings by pointing your toes in and out.

Finish

Perform three to five static stretches of 20 to 30 seconds, or two or three sets of three or four PNF stretches.

STANDING LAT AND PEC STRETCH

The latissimus dorsi and pectorals are two muscle groups that, if not stretched effectively, can restrict range of motion in the shoulder. Flexibility in this area is essential for overall shoulder health, especially for throwing athletes.

Setup

Take a split stance with your left foot forward. Place a ball between your right hand and the wall.

Movement

Begin by rolling the ball straight up the wall until the arm is fully extended. To increase the stretch on the shoulder, lunge forward slightly. Hold the stretch position for 20 to 30 seconds, and return to the original position. You can also perform this dynamically by increasing the speed of the ball roll and lunge.

Finish

Perform three to five static stretches of 20 to 30 seconds or two or three sets of 10 dynamic stretches.

KNEELING POSTERIOR SHOULDER STRETCH

Stretching the posterior side of the shoulder is important for mobility and complete range of motion at the shoulder joint.

Setup

Kneel in front of a ball, with the ball slightly off to the left side. Move your right arm across your body and place it on the ball.

Movement

Begin to roll the ball to the left by pushing with the right hand. As you reach the end of the range, flex forward. This places a greater stretch on the posterior fibers of the deltoid and the rhomboid, which spans the space between your shoulder blade and your upper spine.

Finish

Hold the stretch for 20 to 30 seconds and return to the initial position. Repeat three to five times.

Strength Ball Programs

12

The objective of this 16-week program is to progressively introduce you to the exercises described in the book. For many of you just starting out, there will certainly be a temptation to jump ahead to some of the more difficult exercises, especially if you find some of the beginner-level exercises too easy. But we recommend that you stay on course. Take the time to build your foundation with the progressions we prescribe, and your result will be a successful program. Remember that Rome was not built in a day. The time you put into the program in the first four to six weeks will ensure your success by helping you avoid any potential soft-tissue injuries and reinforcing the techniques as described.

Warm-Up and Movement Preparation

Jumping into your workout without a proper warm-up would not be beneficial to your body. You might be able to relate it to starting your car and immediately trying to drive it on a freezing February morning in Ottawa. You must first start it and then let it warm up so the oil can work its way around the moving engine parts. Your body is no different. Begin by slowly raising your body temperature with five to eight minutes of aerobic activity. Then perform some dynamic activity to lubricate your joints, such as walking lunges, rotating lunges, hip swings, medicine ball ax chops, or robot arms. (These and other dynamic warm-up activities can be found on the accompanying DVD.)

Tempo and Rest

Tempo and rest are two components that can dictate the direction of your program. We'll define the numbers in the tempo column first. For example, 3:2:2 would mean that you lower the weight in 3 seconds, hold the middle position for 2 seconds, and raise the weight in 2 seconds. When a muscle causes a joint to move, it always results in shortening or lengthening of the working muscle. The first digit indicates lowering of the weight, which generally means you put a specific muscle through an eccentric contraction, or lengthening of that muscle. The last digit indicates that you perform a concentric contraction, or shortening of the muscle.

The number in the rest column represents how much time you should take after a particular exercise. The exercises are designed to provide a number of supersets, where one exercise is followed immediately by a second exercise, then followed by a specific rest interval. We use this concept of supersetting as a means of making your workout efficient. Instead of working each muscle individually, we generally use an opposite muscle group (such as chest and upper back) or an upper-body and lower-body combination (such as chest and hamstrings). As you adapt to your program, you can apply the concept of progression to your rest periods to continually increase the intensity of your workouts. By attempting to shorten your rest time you will increase the metabolic intensity of the program, thereby imposing a greater challenge to your body and improving your endurance. You can also increase your rest time, especially if you want to lift very heavy loads. Increasing the rest time will provide you with greater recovery, which is an important component of high-level strength.

Rationale for Program Development

When we design exercise programs for our clients, we take several factors into consideration:

1. The sport the athlete is preparing for
2. Training goals, such as reducing body fat, increasing strength, or increasing muscle mass
3. Chronological age
4. Training age (number of years of resistance and balance training a client has)
5. Injury history
6. Gender
7. Equipment availability (whether or not there is access to the appropriate equipment)

The unfortunate part of designing a program for this book is that we could not get too specific. The design and progressions are carefully planned to provide you with guidelines that will educate you as well as improve your strength. The following are the guidelines that you should use when designing your own program from *Strength Ball Training*.

Stability and balance are addressed from a physiological perspective in chapters 1 and 2. From a programming perspective, stability and balance are characteristics that we prefer to work on early on in our program design. This does not mean we don't do any balance later in the program; rather, the focus might be different. For instance, early on we might focus on unstable balance with a minor strength component, such as the bridge T fall-off in weeks 1 to 4. This exercise allows you to challenge your balance progressively (that is, you dictate your own balance difficulty by how far you laterally roll with the ball). The more you adapt, the farther you will roll. Once you have reached your maximum lateral roll, you could decrease your base of support, which will increase the balance challenge of just being on top of the ball. Bridge Ts are a great introductory balance exercise because you can dictate your difficulty.

The ability to balance in a three-point stance in the Ts will lend itself positively to balance challenges later in the program when there is only a two-point balance, such as the single-leg hip extension and knee flexion. Not only do you have a two-point balance point, but there is also a significant strength requirement during this balance challenge.

We think that the progressions will dictate future success with your program. Without appropriate progressions, results might not occur. Imagine, for instance, you are just starting out with your strength ball program, and you have programmed in the single-leg hip extension and knee flexion in your first cycle. Most people could not perform this exercise effectively because they do not have the required balance or stability. In many cases this failure could result in your quitting the program. Fitness dropout rates are common among people who try to do too much too soon and are turned off by not being able to complete a workout.

When we look at the strength component of programming, the thought processes are very similar to that of balance and stability: Build a base and use reasonable progressions. For instance, you would not want to program the dual-ball fly to work your chest at the beginning of your program. This exercise places great stress on the anterior of the shoulder. It also requires great core stability as you descend into your fly. You will notice that we begin the chest progression by using a bilateral stability ball dumbbell press. This is a great introductory general strength exercise for the pectorals and basic stability exercise for the core. Progress to a unilateral stability ball dumbbell press. This will force the core to work at a much higher level as a result of the unilateral arm movement. After following these progressions for eight weeks, you might be ready to attempt the dual-ball fly. If you cannot descend in a slow, controlled manner while holding your core in the proper position and rise from the low position, you will know that you are not ready for this progression. If that is the case, take a positive step back to reinforce the muscles that will help you achieve success in the movement.

The exercises in this 16-week program provide an excellent array of strength, balance, and flexibility challenges. In most of the 4-week cycles we include captions under the tables explaining why we may have used a specific combination of exercises. Give it a try and examine our logic. After you have completed this program, you will be ready to design your own strength ball program.

Weeks 1 to 4

The first 4 weeks of the program are demonstrated on the DVD.

Exercise	Sets x reps or time	Tempo	Rest period
1a. Wall squat	2-3 x 15-20	3:0:2	0
1b. Static back extension	2-3 x 60 sec	Hold	2 min
2a. Single-leg hip lift	2-3 x 10	2:2:2	0
2b. Dumbbell press	2-3 x 15	3:0:2	1.5 min
3a. Pullover	2-3 x 12	3:2:2	0
3b. Hip extension and knee flexion	2-3 x 12	Slow	1.5 min
4a. McGill static side raise	2-3 x 30 sec	Hold	0
4b. Standing biceps curl	2-3 x 12	3:1:2	1.5 min
5a. Prone balance	2-3 x 30-45 sec	Hold	0
5b. Bridge T fall-off	2-3 x 8-10 to each side	Slow	1.5 min

Finish with the following flexibility exercises, holding each position for 20 to 30 seconds for one or two sets:

1. Spinal extension
2. Lateral side stretch
3. Supine hamstring stretch
4. Standing hamstring stretch
5. Standing lat and pec stretch
6. Kneeling posterior shoulder stretch

Note: In combos 1 and 5 we keep the grouping close together. Superset 1 focuses on legs and glutes in the wall squat and glutes, hamstrings, and spinal erectors in the back extension. This focus on the core and legs is a superset of the same muscle group to enhance hypertrophy and strength of this area. This is a foundation that you need to focus on for later progressions.

In superset 5 the focus is similar to the previous supersets except that we target the abdominals in a sagittal plane followed by a rotary stability challenge—same grouping, different planes.

Weeks 5 to 8

Exercise	Sets x reps or time	Tempo	Rest period
1a. Wall squat with weight	2-3 x 12-15	3:0:2	0
1b. Static back extension	2-3 x 90-120 sec	Hold	2 min
2a. Supine leg cable curl	2-3 x 10	2:2:2	0
2b. One-arm dumbbell press	2-3 x 12	3:0:2	1.5 min
3a. One-arm pullover	2-3 x 12	3:2:2	0
3b. One-leg hip extension and knee flexion	2-3 x 12	Slow	1.5 min
4a. McGill side raise with static hip adduction	2-3 x 10-12	2:1:2	0
4b. Standing biceps curl	2-3 x 10	3:1:2	1.5 min
5a. Prone balance hip opener	2-3 x 10	Slow	0
5b. Bridge with medicine ball drop	2-3 x 10-12	Fast	1.5 min

Finish with the following flexibility exercises, holding each position for 20 to 30 seconds for one or two sets:

1. Spinal extension
2. Lateral side stretch
3. Supine hamstring stretch
4. Standing hamstring stretch
5. Standing lat and pec stretch
6. Kneeling posterior shoulder stretch

Weeks 9 to 12

Exercise	Sets x reps or time	Tempo	Rest period
1a. Single-leg wall squat	2-3 x 6-8	2:0:2	0
1b. Reverse back extension	2-3 x 8-12	3:0:3	2 min
2a. One-leg hip extension and knee flexion	2-3 x 8-10	Slow	0
2b. Dual-ball fly	2-3 x 8-12	3:0:2	1.5 min
3a. Cross-body rear delt raise	2-3 x 10-12	3:2:2	0
3b. Prone row external rotation	2-3 x 10-12	3:1:2	1.5 min
4a. Kneeling hold and clock	2-3 x 30-60 sec	Hold	0
4b. Incline triceps extension	2-3 x 12	3:0:2	1.5 min
5a. Jackknife	2-3 x 10-15	2:2:2	0
5b. Twister	2-3 x 10-12	Slow	1.5 min

Finish with the following flexibility exercises, holding each position for 20 to 30 seconds for one or two sets:

1. Spinal extension
2. Lateral side stretch
3. Supine hamstring stretch
4. Standing hamstring stretch
5. Standing lat and pec stretch
6. Kneeling posterior shoulder stretch

Note: As you progress into week 9 you increase the intensity through several methods. For the legs, progress to unilateral squats, which are significantly more difficult than bilateral movements for the legs. The movements are multidirectional and therefore harder to stabilize, and the loading on the legs also changes. We also superset a chest and hamstring exercise. Both are considered advanced level. This combination will significantly increase the metabolic challenge as well as the strength challenge.

Weeks 13 to 16

Exercise	Sets x reps or time	Tempo	Rest period
1a. Overhead lateral medicine ball squat	2-3 x 8-12	3:0:2	0
1b. Poor man's glute ham raise rollout	2-3 x 8-10	Slow	2 min
2a. Supine lat pull and delt raise	2-3 x 8-10	Slow	0
2b. Walking lunge and rotate	2-3 x 10-12	3:0:2	1.5 min
3a. Supine dumbbell press and fly	2-3 x 10-12	2:0:2	0
3b. Supine scissors	2-3 x 10-12	2:0:2	1.5 min
4a. Wrap sit-up	2-3 x 12-15 sec	3:0:2	0
4b. Medicine ball push-up	2-3 x 12	2:0:2	1.5 min
5a. Prone lat pull	2-3 x 10-12	2:2:2	0
5b. Goldy's static helicopter	2-3 x 10-12	Slow	1.5 min

Finish with the following flexibility exercises, holding each position for 20 to 30 seconds for one or two sets:

1. Spinal extension
2. Lateral side stretch
3. Supine hamstring stretch
4. Standing hamstring stretch
5. Standing lat and pec stretch
6. Kneeling posterior shoulder stretch

Note: In the final cycle the exercises progress to very advanced. Most notably we introduce the challenge of contralateral movements within the same exercise for the supine lat pull and delt raise, and we introduce the concept of working the same muscle but with different movements from one side to the other with the supine dumbbell press and fly.

References

Anderson, K., and D.G. Behm. 2005. Impact of instability resistance training on balance and stability. *Sports Medicine* 35(1): 43-53.

Behm, D.G., A.M. Leonard, W.B. Yound, W.A. Bonsey, and S.N. MacKinnon. 2005. Trunk muscle electromyographic activity with unstable and unilateral exercises. *Journal of Strength and Conditioning Research* 19(1): 193-201.

Berg, K. 1989. Balance and its measure in the elderly: A review. *Physiotherapy* 41: 240-246.

Cholewicki, J., and S.M. McGill. 1996. Mechanical stability of the in vivo lumbar spine: Implications for injury and chronic low back pain. *Clinical Biomechanics* 11(1): 1-15.

Chu, D. 1992. *Jumping into plyometrics.* Champaign, IL: Leisure Press.

Irrgang, J., S.L. Whitney, and E.D. Cox. 1994. Balance and proprioceptive training for rehabilitation of the lower extremity. *Journal of Sport Rehabilitation* 3: 68-83.

Lephart, S., D.M. Pincivero, J.L. Giraldo, and F.H. Fu. 1997. The role of proprioception in the management and rehabilitation of athletic injuries. *American Journal of Sports Medicine* 25(1): 130-137.

Lephart, S., C.B. Swanik, and T. Boonriong. 1998. Anatomy and physiology of proprioception and neuromuscular control. *Athletic Therapy Today* 3(5): 6-9.

McGill, S. 1997. The biomechanics of low back injury: Implications on current practice in industry and the clinic. *Journal of Biomechanics* 30(5): 465-475.

McGill, S. 1998. Low back exercises: Evidence for improving exercise regimens. *Physical Therapy* 78(7): 754-765.

McGill, S. 2002. *Low back disorders.* Champaign, IL: Human Kinetics.

Posner-Mayer, J. 1995. *Swiss ball applications for orthopedic and sports medicine: A guide for home exercise programs utilizing the Swiss ball.* Denver, CO: Ball Dynamics International.

Richardson, C., G. Jull, P. Hodges, and J. Hides. 1999. *Therapeutic exercise for spinal segmental stabilization in low back pain.* London: Churchill Livingstone.

Santana, J.C. 2005. Biomechanical comparison of the one-arm standing press and bench press including muscle response. Abstract presentation. Las Vegas: NSCA National Conference.

Twist, P. 1997. *Complete conditioning for ice hockey.* Champaign IL, Human Kinetics.

Wirhed, R. 1990. *Athletic ability and the anatomy of motion.* London: Wolfe Medical.

Are you on the ball? For more info...

www.strengthballexercises.com

Visit the authors at www.strengthballexercises.com,
your complete resource for:

▸ New exercises
▸ Real workout video clips
▸ Pro coach tips
▸ Win prizes
▸ CEC products
▸ Share your success story!

About the Authors

Lorne Goldenberg has worked as a strength and conditioning coach for the Florida Panthers, Ottawa Senators Hockey Club, St. Louis Blues, Chicago Blackhawks, Quebec Nordiques, Colorado Avalanche, Windsor Spitfires, and the Ottawa 67s. He lectures internationally on a variety of topics, including stability ball exercises and ground-based sports conditioning, for such groups as the National Strength and Conditioning Association, Society of Weight Training Injury Specialists, provincial associations, and professional teams. He has written for the NSCA *Journal of Strength and Conditioning, Ironman, Physical, Men's Journal, Hockey Life,* and *Hockey Now.*

Goldenberg is the president of Strength Tek Fitness & Wellness Consultants, which provides workplace health and wellness programs across Canada (www.strengthtek.com). He also is the president of the Athletic Conditioning Center, which is Ottawa's only sport conditioning facility for the serious athlete (www.accottawa.com). He lives in Ottawa, Ontario, with his children, Isaak and Danielle.

Peter Twist is the former strength and conditioning coach for the Vancouver Canucks and is currently president of Twist Conditioning Incorporated (www.sportconditioning.com), an athlete conditioning company with athlete conditioning centers; one-on-one and team training; a line of 350 sport fitness products; and sport conditioning specialist certifications delivered by Twist Master Coaches throughout Canada, the United States, Australia, and the United Kingdom. A frequent guest lecturer at international fitness conferences and coaching clinics, Twist delivers workshops on sport conditioning to personal trainers, conditioning coaches, sport coaches, teachers and medical professionals around the globe.

Twist has authored 7 books, 16 DVDs, and over 400 articles on functional training. He also provides exercise information via home study to athletes, parents, and exercise professionals in several countries.

An NSCA-certified strength and conditioning specialist with a master's degree in coaching science from the University of British Columbia, Twist served as president of the Hockey Conditioning Coaches Association, editor of the *Journal of Hockey Conditioning,* and NSCA provincial director for British Columbia. Twist lives in North Vancouver with his wife Julie, daughters Zoe and Mackenzie, and dogs Rico and Loosy.

AUG 0 2 2011